INDEX

Chapter 1: The Search for Meaning

When the questions arise, "What is our purpose on Earth?" as this is not a personal quest but the universal one to know about the role we're playing in our lives.

Yes, we learn from the others regarding different types of things like different cultures, human experience, clarity over certain values, and direction to our lives. Now learning is a part of our lives to explore and understand what is right or wrong. Some believe in listening, some in watching, but the actual belief is to feel correct. Beliefs are often formed through personal experience, upbringing by family, religious influences, socialization, and education and learning.

Identifying our role of service and contribution to others. Always serve others, live with kindness, and be a better example for the people. Respecting doesn't make you weak, nor will you get anything by disrespecting others, and that is how you make a more meaningful and fulfilling life for ourselves and others. Once we have a clearer sense of our purpose, our perspective towards the things, pure intentions, and making choices that reflect to make this world better. The journey to understand and overcome our fear, doubt, and problem. It's not easy to practice these things suddenly but slowly with the support from our inner self and the person who's there to make changes to this world. One day the earth will be better and more beautiful for the people living on it. We have to observe everything around us; we will definitely find out who we are and what's our role in this world ahead while reading the chapters of this book.

Chapter 2: Human Impact on the planet

Humans are born to live in peace, but the devil changes it all by manipulating everything a person cares about. Sometimes we're not in control of what we're doing. Our brain and body listen to a creature that is not even real and created by the imagination of humans or curse evil spirits.

We're the reason for many problems currently Earth is facing, like global warming, deforestation, pollution, dirty oceans and rivers, etc. These all come from human mistakes, and even people are hurting by mental crises. Humans are getting ill with various diseases that totally depend upon the surroundings and environment. They don't believe in taking care of ourselves rather than eating anything just for fun or to taste good. What people learn for this mentally is to don't care about what is going around; surely other people will take it, make it clean, or correct it. Our evil thought teaches us this all: to deny social equality between people. Everything is not in fortune in everyone's life. People do listen, but unfortunately only some understand. Change the world by removing hate from inside you. It's not easy to digest to believe in someone you don't like. Humans need to practice their impact over everything they're involved in; even after all these, something will definitely miss, and somehow people will find mistakes by listening to inside evil, as said above. Unfortunately, the only thing that can save humans from these problems is not blindly believing what they hear or see; they either do search and find faith.

Chapter 3: Building Trust on Someone

When people don't trust the truth of meaningful relationships, they doubt things they don't know because anyone can tell the lie. As humans are both positive and negative mindset, they mostly listen to their evil imagination, which can benefit them, and don't think about the others. A bitter truth is that people often judge others on the basis of what they don't like and don't consider themselves to society, but the reality is, if you don't get them right on what wrong they are doing, how will they look for you and build trust in you? Making boundaries is okay, but ignoring something you can improve towards to change the world, that's definitely not correct.

The amazing thing about trust is that it cannot be established without effectiveness; it cannot be bought. Whoever understands things will listen to others; the better you listen, the more understand to believe in something. You have to know the purpose before trusting anyone, and you need to provide your perspective towards the findings. Always make sure that your answer doesn't degrade or hurt anyone; better yet, you can take your time before speaking immediately for a good conclusion. A way to placing confidence in another person, as trust is not given lightly; it's earned through your behaviour and actions. Never hesitate to apologize to someone to whom you have broken their trust. Heal the damage you have done and be clear and honest before expecting someone's firm belief; that's the right way you can rebuild trust. These take many things to look after all, and more you will learn about this when you are understood.

Chapter 4: Human with Technologies

The technology is growing around all over the world. Some people still don't know how to use it, and some are tired of using it. The impact of technologies will be bigger than we think; nowadays it becomes our daily norm from the moment we wake up to the time we go to bed in the night. Technology plays a vital role in shaping how we live, work, and interact with others. The more benefits it brings, the more dangerous it will become for the people.

As technology continues to evolve, humans are adapting to new techniques, tools, and ways of living towards balancing benefits and risks. The technology revolution is a must because it provides much information, communication, ease of life, etc. While discussing this thing, we're getting everything we want, but looking to the other side, somewhat technology is damaging to the human brain as people are getting addicted to it. They're affected by mental health issues, anxiety, and depression. People are learning some unnecessary things from the social media and wasting time into that they think it's important for them.

More affecting people of this social media addiction are the teenagers. They were in the age of learning and dealing with different conditions, but most of them get depressed for something that is not even the reality which do injury to their mental peace and get attracted to mental trauma. Life is miserable for them as they can't decide what to do and get things messy for themselves. This topic is more than you thought and will continue on the next page of this book, where something new you will identify.

Everyone gets busy with technology because it's attracting people more, and younger people are more involved in this due to a desire for something that's harmful for them. By quoting this, it doesn't mean everything is wrong with technology, but on the other hand, the data everyone shares on different platforms has been used by many applications and websites that recommend the things in which you're interested, everything you search for, and everything you share on different social media platforms. Not everyone wants to interfere with your privacy, but from chapter 2, there is always an evil mind who knows, any can blackmail you with your personal information, even if you have never done any wrong thing. Here, artificial intelligence comes in, and you can't imagine what can happen to your privacy. People with bad intentions harass and blame you for things you've never done; even your close ones don't listen to you because mostly people believe what they see, where listening becomes less to trust.

Using technology and AI, people will fraud in the name of innocence to show something and make you believe in that which is totally fake. Your location can be tracked and misused to do something wrong with you because hate is born with the disagreeing right and an evil mind. This AI makes you and others to judge between reality and social life. The moral is that people will potentially misuse your data, which can lead to privacy violations and biased decision-making. Always remember, the more you use technology carefully, the more raising concerns will decrease. Perhaps this doesn't suddenly stop; after all, sharing your data everywhere isn't right, and you will understand and get to know it in the future.

Chapter 5: Voices for Change

What equality teaches is that each individual has equal rights, opportunities, and treatment regardless of their background. By this statement, everything seems good until it's applied to the world.

People here are living in inequality, but when coming to this topic more somewhat, every creature on the earth is born to play a different role. Justice should be the same for everyone; it's only work when you take a fair decision and make an make an equitable distribution of words, resources, opportunities, and responsibilities.

Equality can be brought about by ensuring that everyone has equal access to education, treatment, and opportunities. Progress makes the world better, but many societies still face the issue where income inequality, racial discrimination, and gender-based violence remain significant challenges. It's important to promote equality when government, organization, and individual play a crucial role in implementing policies that provide justice to everyone. Social justice and equality are not only moral imperatives but also essential elements for building a sustainable and harmonious world. By championing these principles, individuals and societies can work towards creating a future where every person can live with dignity, freedom, and opportunity.

Always make sure we heard to the unbiased decision taken the higher authority and make them correct by providing the right option for social justice and equality.

Chapter 6: Seeds of Growth

Once you get comfortable feeling uncomfortable, then your growth is unlimited. Our journey through life is marked by moments of learning, overcoming challenges, and striving for a better future for ourselves and those around us.

Imagine a young girl in a small village who dreams of becoming a doctor. Despite limited resources, she studies by the dim of a kerosene lamp, fueled by her passion and determination. Each book she reads, every test she takes, and all the obstacles she overcomes bring her one step closer to her dream. It's about setting goals, learning from our failures, and celebrating our successes. Whether it's learning a new skill, overcoming a personal fear, or achieving a long-held aspiration, every step we take in our personal growth journey enriches our lives.

Now, consider the story of a community coming together to build a school in an underserved area. The collective effort of parents, teachers, and volunteers creates a space where children can learn, dream, and aspire. It's about more than bricks and mortar it's about providing opportunities, fostering hope, and creating a brighter future. Through these efforts, we build a world where everyone has the opportunity to succeed.

The road to growth and development is not always smooth. We face challenges such as economic inequality, environmental degradation, and political instability. But it's the moments of adversity that our true strength shines.

Each of us has a role to play in this journey. We can create a world where everyone thrives. It's about lifting each other up, sharing knowledge, and working together towards common goals. So, whether you're a student, a professional, a parent, or a community leader, remember that your efforts matter. Every positive change you make, no matter how small, contributes to the greater good. Together, we can inspire a brighter future for the people on earth where growth and development are not just goals but realities for all.

When we come together with compassion, innovation, and a shared vision for a better world, we ignite a spark of hope that has the potential to illuminate the path forward for generations to come. By believing in ourselves and each other, we can turn dreams into reality and build a future where growth and development are the cornerstones of an equitable society. Develop ourselves as much as you can, indeed it's hard and challenging but what makes you better, stronger and independent. Keep motivate yourself even if you don't want anything for yourself but you can make the difference to others life.

Growth is temporary for some people as some point in their life it won't expand but the impact someone can makes is much powerful.

Chapter 7: The Future of Humanity

If things will go like this only, we people definitely face such an issue no one is able to cure. There are many impacts that will harm humans on earth, like climate change, overuse of technologies towards addiction, and unequal access to different things. We know many things will improve, but more will worsen as per the current situation. Our planet is experiencing rapid changes causing extreme heatwaves, storms, and rising sea levels. These changes are not just environmental; they're affecting our health, economy, and communities. The recent pandemic has shown us how interconnected and vulnerable we are, highlighting the need for resilience and adaptability. While technology offers incredible opportunities, it also brings challenges, such as increased screen time, social media addiction, and the erosion of face-to-face interactions. These issues can impact relationships, and overall well-being. We have to take some steps to improve before it can be worsened, like reducing waste, conserving energy, and supporting eco-friendly products, which can make a difference. Support policies that protect the environment and make a difference by stopping people who are causing this more. For technology addiction, you have to engage in hobbies, prioritize face-to-face interactions, set boundaries for screen time, spend time in nature, and foster real-world connections to help maintain a healthy balance.

The future of humanity is shaped by our choices and actions today. We can create a world that reflects our values of sustainability, equity, and progress. As we navigate the uncertainties ahead, let us remain hopeful and committed to building a future where every person has the opportunity to thrive and contribute to a better world.

Chapter 8: Evolution of Consciousness

It is said that what makes us human is the essence of consciousness. In many regards, this is taken to be a major innate part existing within our inner world: where thoughts, emotions, and memory reside. It enables self-reflection on the past, imagine the future, and making decisions for our present. Consciousness, however, cannot be reduced solely to personal awareness; it's a relation between us and the larger universe. This is one of the deepest segments in the evolution of human consciousness. In the earlier periods was mainly concerned with the rise of issues regarding primary survival: how to find food and shelter, how to protect oneself from calamities and enemies, etc. now we more protect ourselves from hackers not the thief. As societies and cultural development went on, so also did the minds of humans, it spread into deeper and wider dimensions with all subtle thoughts, emotions, and social interactions.

Modern life pulsates with change; significant changes are happening in the way we think and regard reality. One of the more striking domains of change in everyday life has to be credited to the advancements in technology. The tremendous inflows of information it brought along did not end there but rather opened floodgates to social media connections. Problems spawned by technology include an excess of information and a lack of thoughtfulness. To remain well-grounded, one will have to feel and exercise mindfulness, be wary of spurious information, and critically assess what one consumes.

The more our awareness stretches to hold global issues such as climate change and social justice, the more our consciousness expands. This shift in consciousness makes people more compassionate and interested in what happens in the world around them; this creates an urge to make good, socially responsive choices. Lastly, many people are turning inward, exploring spirituality and self-reflection as a way to deepen their understanding of themselves and their place in the universe. This inner growth helps us connect more deeply with others and the world around us, fostering a more compassionate and aware way of living.

The evolution of man offers much promise for the future of consciousness. Maybe this will be the time for the shift into collective consciousness, with guiding principles like empathy, compassion, and cooperation toward more peaceful and just societies. It may perhaps also embody transcendence from individual identities and foster deeper unity with the planet, other beings, and the universe.

It could make a difference in enhancing our mental and emotional well-being, in surmounting global challenges, and in strengthening our bonds with one another as humankind marches on in its development. The future of consciousness is, at the end, about growing our personal and collective awareness towards a world, were deeper understanding and connection drive progress and well-being.

Chapter 9: The Endless Quest

The most powerful instruments we have to frame our destinies are education. It's not merely about getting information or abilities for employment rather education is a process of growing into people and societies throughout the whole life. In a rapidly changing world of today, it has never been more crucial than before to keep learning all the time since every day presents new challenges as well as opportunities.

As we think about it that growth mindset is premised on the belief that abilities and intelligence can be developed through effort, learning, and perseverance. It helps us view challenges not as obstacles to be overcome, but rather as opportunities for learning and growth.

Learning isn't just for the young. Whether you're 8 or 80, there's always something new to learn. Lifelong learning keeps the mind active, promotes mental and emotional well-being, and helps us stay engaged with the world around us.

As we look to the future, it's clear that the need for education and lifelong learning will only continue to grow. To thrive in an ever-changing world, we must cultivate a culture that values and supports continuous learning. This means recognizing the importance of both formal and informal education, encouraging curiosity and creativity, and providing access to learning opportunities for people of all ages and backgrounds.

Chapter 10: Nurturing Body and Mind

When we talk about health, it's easy to think that our physical body will stay free of illness, we eat right food, and exercising regularly. However, true well-being encompasses much more. It includes mental, emotional, and social health, all of which are interconnected and essential for a fulfilling life.

All we know that in today's fast-paced world, maintaining health and well-being can be challenging. The pressures of work, family, and social obligations often leave just a little time for self-care. Additionally, the constant of information from technology and media can overwhelm our senses and contribute to anxiety.

Physical health is about more than just the absence of disease. It's about maintaining a balanced, active lifestyle that supports all body functions have to maintain properly. Make conscious choices to nourish your body. Eat a balanced diet of fruits, vegetables, lean proteins, and whole grains. Prioritize sleep and practice good sleep hygiene, as rest is crucial for overall health. Mental and emotional health refers to how we think, feel, and cope with life. It's about finding balance, managing stress, and cultivating a positive outlook. Sometimes we get offended for something, we don't have to care about. Emotional well-being also includes having healthy relationships and feeling connected to others. Take care of your mind by practicing mindfulness, meditation, or other relaxation techniques that help reduce stress and anxiety. Stay connected with friends and family, and don't hesitate to seek support if you're struggling emotionally.

I know some challenges we face like the demands of work can often encroach on personal time, making it difficult to find a healthy balance. This imbalance can lead to burnout, stress, and a decline in overall well-being.

Also, while technology connects us and provides valuable information, it can also lead to overstimulation and reduced face-to-face interactions. The constant presence of screens and social media can impact our mental health and disrupt sleep.

Set boundaries between work and personal life. Make time for activities that recharge you, whether it's spending time with loved ones, pursuing hobbies, or simply relaxing. Practice digital mindfulness by setting limits on screen time and being mindful of how technology affects your mood and energy levels. Take breaks from screens, especially before bedtime, and prioritize in-person interactions whenever possible.

At the end health and well-being are about much more than just avoiding illness they're about living a balanced, fulfilling life. By taking a holistic approach that considers physical, mental, emotional, and social health, we can create a foundation for lifelong well-being. As we navigate the complexities of modern life, it's important to remember that small, consistent steps can lead to big changes. create a healthier, happier future for ourselves and those around us.

Chapter 11: The Spark of New Ideas

As innovation and creativity both are the heartbeat of human development. These enable us to imagine new possibilities, solve problems, and make life better for ourselves and future generations. From the tiny spark of an idea to a brilliant discovery, creativity shapes how we understand the world and respond to challenges. It's not about artists or inventors instead everyone has the capacity for creativity in their own unique way.

Innovation takes creativity and turns it into action. It's approximately looking at antique problems with fresh eyes and finding new, efficient methods to remedy them.

Throughout history, innovations have improved how we live whether it's through technology, medicine, or new forms of communication. But instead, what we have to learn the proper use of our creative to invest at right place. The internet, smartphones, renewable energy solutions, and medical advances all stem from the innovative thinking of people who dared to push the limits of what we know.

We can all nurture our creativity by engaging in new experiences, learning continuously, and collaborating with others. When we combine imagination with persistence, we create opportunities for growth, innovation, and positive change. By embracing these qualities, we can tackle the challenges of today and shape a better future.

Chapter 12: Threads of Connection

While discussing about this topic people don't know exactly what it's? but if we look into love and relationships are the essence of what it means to be human. They shape who we are, how we see the world, and how we connect with others. Love is more than just a feeling; it's a powerful force that binds people together through trust, care, and understanding.

At the heart of every relationship is connection. We thrive when we feel seen, heard, and valued by those we care about as love is not finding the right person instead love is what becoming the right person. Love allows us to be vulnerable, to grow, and to feel supported, no matter the ups and downs of life.

There's something profoundly beautiful about connecting with another person. At its core, love is about understanding and being understood, seeing and being seen. It's the quiet moments of companionship, the shared laughter, the comfort in times of pain. Love bridges the gap between individuals, allowing us to experience life not alone but with someone by our side. They require care, patience, and, most of all, a willingness to give and receive. It's not about perfection, but about commitment: showing up for each other, listening without judgment, and supporting each other through both the good and difficult times. True love accepts flaws and imperfections and transforms them into opportunities for deeper understanding.

At its core, love is about growth. It invites us to grow individually and together. It pushes us to face our fears, embrace our imperfections, and stretch beyond our comfort zones. In a loving relationship, we find the courage to be our true selves, knowing we are accepted just as we are.

Ultimately, love is the heart of life. It turns ordinary moments into extraordinary memories, bringing meaning and depth to our existence. Whether it's the tenderness of a quiet conversation, the joy in a shared adventure, or the comfort of simply being together, love is what makes life richer, fuller, and more beautiful.

At last, these remind us that we are never truly alone. In a world that can sometimes feel overwhelming, love anchors us, giving us the strength to face challenges and the joy of celebrating life together. It is through our relationships that we find meaning, purpose, and the deepest form of happiness. Choose your love every day because isn't something you find instead it's something that finds you.

Chapter 13: Building the Dream

Work and career are central to our lives, shaping not only how we spend our days but also how we perceive ourselves and contribute to the world. In many ways, our jobs give structure to life, from the starch to fully prepared that providing both challenges and rewards. However, work should be more than just a routine it should offer a sense of purpose.

At its core, work is about more than earning money. It's about finding something meaningful to do with our time and understand certain things to get involve into with what you have something that resonates with our passions, talents, and values. When we feel connected to the work we do, it becomes fulfilling, energizing, and a source of pride. This doesn't mean that every job will always feel perfect, but discovering how our work contributes to a greater good or aligns with our personal goals can make even the toughest tasks feel worthwhile.

Work can be demanding, and no career comes without its share of difficulties. Whether it's stress, uncertainty, or setbacks, everyone faces obstacles at some point. The key is learning to adapt, grow, and don't let these challenges define us. Flexibility is essential being open to change and viewing difficulties as opportunities for growth helps us stay resilient. It's important to remember that failure is not the end; it's part of the learning process. The only way to do great work is to love what you do.

When you find yourself feeling overwhelmed or unsure about your path, taking time to reflect on what's important to you can help. Sometimes, the challenges we face are signals that we need a shift, either in how we approach our work or in the direction of our career.

Work should be an important part of life, but it shouldn't be everything. Finding balance is crucial for our life and emotional well-being. This means setting boundaries, knowing when to rest, and making time for personal relationships and activities that bring joy outside of work. It's easy to get caught up in the rush of work, but true success is found in a life where we have time for both productivity and relaxation.

Balance is about recognizing that we are more than our jobs. We need space for family, friends, hobbies, and self-care. In a world that often glorifies overworking, finding time to rest and recharge is essential to long-term happiness and success.

Careers are no longer a straight path. In today's world, things change quickly, and we must be ready to grow and adapt. This means continually learning new skills and being open to new experiences. Whether it's taking a course, exploring a new interest, or learning from colleagues, growth is a key part of maintaining a fulfilling career.

By approaching our work with purpose and perspective, we can create a path that brings both success and personal satisfaction, allowing us to thrive both professionally and personally.

Chapter 14: Freedom of Fulfillment

It's not about reaching towards always plan to desire for something, is not a constant high or an absence of problems. It is a deep sense of contentment, a recognition of the beauty and goodness that already exist in life. Many people chase happiness in future goals, thinking they'll be happy "when" they get a promotion, make more money, or achieve certain milestones. However, happiness isn't something to be chased; it's something to be experienced in the present moment.

Gratitude plays a significant role in happiness. By appreciating the small moments, the simple joys in everyday life, we can cultivate happiness regardless of external circumstances. It's about being mindful of what we already have, rather than focusing on what's missing.

And when we talk about fulfillment as it's different from happiness. While happiness is about how we feel, fulfillment is about how we live. It's the sense of purpose and meaning that comes from aligning our actions with our core values. Fulfillment happens when we do things that matter to us, when we contribute to something bigger than ourselves, and when we are able to express our true selves. People often find fulfillment in relationships, creative pursuits, personal growth, or contributing to the well-being of others. Fulfillment is a long-term journey, not something achieved overnight. It requires self-awareness, reflection, and the courage to make choices that are true to who we are, even when those choices are difficult.

One of the biggest barriers to both happiness and fulfillment is the constant comparison to others. In the digital age, we are bombarded with images of other people's lives, which can make us feel like we are falling short. It's important to remember that everyone's journey is different, and true happiness and fulfillment come from within, not from measuring up to others.

Another barrier is the belief that happiness and fulfillment are the same for everyone. Each person must define what happiness and fulfillment mean for themselves. For some, it might mean success in a career; for others, it could be close relationships, personal growth, or a balance of different aspects of life. The key is finding what resonates with you personally.

Happiness and fulfillment are deeply interconnected. Happiness can be fleeting, but fulfillment offers a deeper, more enduring sense of satisfaction. However, by aligning our daily lives with our values, and by embracing the present moment while pursuing meaningful goals, we can experience both happiness and fulfillment.

Journeys that each person must navigate in their own way. It's not about perfection or having it all figured out, it's about embracing the present, staying true to ourselves, and finding joy and meaning in the everyday moments that make life beautiful.

As far so we have connected with different topic related to our life and measuring about what need to be improve in ourselves.

Chapter 15: The Morality of Choice

Ethics and morality are the invisible frameworks that guide human behavior, shaping how we interact with the world and with one another. They form the foundation of what it means to live a good life, to do what is right, and to respect others. While every culture and individual may have their own interpretation of ethical values, the universal principles of fairness, honesty, empathy, and justice remain at the heart of human existence.

In today's world, ethical dilemmas are more visible and complex than ever. From issues related to business practices, and global crises to personal challenges in relationships and work, we constantly face choices that challenge our ethics and morality. We think as our mind adapted to it but actually, we can't maintain our action to be right.

One of the most powerful tools in navigating ethical decisions is empathy. Empathy allows us to put ourselves in others' shoes, to understand their feelings, and to see the world from their perspective. When we approach situations with empathy, we are more likely to make decisions that are kind, fair, and just. It fosters a sense of shared humanity and reminds us that, regardless of our differences, we are all connected and our actions have a ripple effect on the lives of others.

In a world that is increasingly driven by individual success and competition, ethics and morality remind us of our responsibility to others. As we continue to face moral challenges in an increasingly complex world, the importance of empathy, fairness, and integrity cannot be overstated. By living with a strong ethical foundation, we contribute to a world that is more compassionate, just, and respectful of the human experience.

Chapter 16: Exploring the Unknown

Life itself is an adventure, a journey filled with discovery, growth, and moments that take us beyond the familiar. But adventure is not just about traveling to new places; it's about stepping outside our comfort zones, embracing the unknown, and seeing life as a continuous experience of observing new things. Adventure is a mindset, one that embraces curiosity and the willingness to face uncertainty. It's about seeing the world with fresh eyes, finding beauty in unexpected places, and welcoming challenges as opportunities for growth.

The Earth itself is a playground for adventure. From the highest mountains to the deepest oceans, every corner of the planet offers a unique experience. Yet, adventure is not just about the physical journey, it's also about self-discovery. As we explore new places and meet new people, we learn more about who we are and what we're capable of. When we embrace adventure, we invite transformation. Adventure often brings us face-to-face with challenges and uncertainties that force us to grow. It helps us develop resilience, adaptability, and a deeper understanding of the world and ourselves. We become more open-minded and empathetic, better able to navigate life's complexities.

Through adventure, we learn to trust ourselves and the process of life. We may not always know where the journey will take us, but each step teaches us something valuable and keeps us curious, engaged, and continuously learning, pushing us to live life fully. The Earth is full of possibilities, and the adventure is yours to create.

Chapter 17: Strength in Struggle

Challenges are an inevitable part of life. They come in various form like personal setbacks, professional struggles, or unexpected life events but they all share one thing: the potential to shape us into stronger, more resilient individuals. How we deal with dare by transforming obstacles into opportunities for learning and self-improvement.

It's important to remember that challenges don't define us, how we respond to them does? While it's easy to feel overwhelmed, maintaining a perspective that every challenge is a stepping stone can help shift our focus from defeat to growth. Instead of asking, "Why is this happening to me?" we can ask, "What can I learn from this?"

Learning from Failure

Failure is often seen as something to be feared, but it is one of the greatest teachers. Every time we fail, we gain valuable insights about ourselves and the world around us. Instead of letting failure discourage us, we can use it as a tool for growth, analyzing what went wrong and how we can improve next time.

Learning from failure also means being kind to ourselves. Mistakes are part of being human, and no one is immune to them. The key is to approach failure with humility and a willingness to learn. By doing so, we turn setbacks into setups.

Provocation is part of the fabric of life, but they don't have to break us. The true measure of our character is not in how we avoid challenges, but in how we rise to meet them.

Chapter 18: Leaving a Mark

Yes, legacy is a reflection of what matters most to us. It's not where we limit to wealth or possessions but includes our values, ideals, and the positive influence we impart on others. Legacy can be as simple as instilling kindness in the hearts of those around us, raising children with love and integrity, or sharing knowledge and experiences to inspire future generations. What you leave behind is not what is engraved in stone monuments, but what is woven into the lives of others.

To define our legacy, we must first understand what we want to stand for. What do we hope people will remember about us? What values do we want to pass on? Taking the time to reflect on these questions helps us to prove actions with our ideals, ensuring that we live with purpose and intention.

Sometimes, we may think that a legacy has to be grand impactful. But often, it's the small, everyday actions that have the most profound effect. Acts of kindness, moments of empathy, and simple gestures of support can resonate deeply with others, creating a ripple effect that extends beyond what we can see. By touching the lives of those around us, we can create a legacy of compassion, generosity, and love.

Every interaction holds the potential to make a positive impact. By being mindful of how we treat others, we contribute to a more caring and respectful world. When we strive to make even small positive changes in our own lives, we inspire others to do the same, sparking a chain reaction of goodwill that endures long after we're gone.

To leave a meaningful legacy, it's essential to live with purpose. This means finding out the meaning of what we're here for and what impact we can create to the world. Living with purpose helps us focus on what truly matters, allowing us to build a legacy of integrity and authenticity.

While our lives are finite, the impact we make can be timeless. Contributing to causes we care about, mentoring others, and sharing our experiences can create lasting change. Whether it's through volunteer work, advocating for social justice, or helping others develop their skills and potential, we have the power to create a legacy that continues to make a difference.

To make a lasting impact, we can also focus on leaving behind something tangible, such as a work of art, a charitable foundation, or a project that benefits future generations. But most importantly, we can leave behind intangible gifts like hope, knowledge, and encouragement that empower others to build their own legacies.

Legacy and impact remind us that our lives are part of something greater than ourselves. By living with intention, showing compassion, and acting in alignment with our values, we contribute to a world that reflects the best of who we are. The legacy we leave behind is not just in what we achieve, but in how we touch and make the world a little better. We may be here for a finite time, but the mark we leave on the hearts of those we've inspired endures, shaping a future that carries forward our hopes, dreams, and ideals.

Chapter 19: Impact of Our Sudden Action

In life, we all make sudden decisions, act on impulse, or respond emotionally to situations. These moments can often lead to unintended consequences, sometimes positive, but also sometimes regrettable. Understanding the impact of our sudden actions is crucial because we don't know what if others hurt or not. See how we view ourselves, and how we leave a lasting mark on the world around us.

Every action we take creates a ripple effect, influencing not just ourselves but also those around us. A kind word said in the heat of the moment can lift someone's spirits, while a thoughtless comment can deeply wound. Similarly, a hasty financial decision might lead to unexpected debt, or an impulsive career choice might set us on an unplanned path. Recognizing the power of these ripples helps us understand the weight of our actions. Even small decisions can trigger chains of events that shape our lives and the lives of others in meaningful ways. By being aware of the potential outcomes of our actions, we can approach each situation with greater mindfulness and responsibility.

Life will always have moments that call for quick decisions, and spontaneity has its place in bringing excitement and discovery. However, balancing spontaneity with responsibility allows us to embrace the moment while being mindful of the broader impact. This means knowing when to follow our instincts and when to take a step back to consider the possible outcomes.

Striking this balance enables us to live fully and authentically while honouring our responsibilities to ourselves, others, and the world around us. By blending spontaneity with thoughtfulness, we can enjoy the richness of the present without compromising the integrity of our future.

Chapter 20: Seeing Beyond the Surface

This topic is what we want to discuss often as perspective shapes how we see the world, how we interpret our experiences, and ultimately, how we live our lives. It's the lens through which we view everything around us, and it can either limit us or open up new possibilities.

Our emotional responses are often tied to how we perceive events. A negative experience can feel overwhelming, but changing our perspective can reduce its emotional weight. Instead of focusing on what went wrong, we can focus on the lessons learned or strength gained from overcoming. It's sometimes the perspective we judge people wrong instead of making them correct. The way we interpret experiences shapes our emotional landscape, and in turn, our overall well-being.

One of the greatest benefits of a shift in perspective is how it impacts our relationships. When we take the time to see things from someone else's point of view, we become more understanding and less judgmental. Conflicts often arise because we're stuck in our own perspective, unable to appreciate where the other person is coming from.

Perspective has the power to transform not only how we see the world but how we live in it. When we realize that we can control our viewpoint, we gain the ability to shape our own reality. Life's challenges become less daunting when we approach them with a mindset that focuses on growth and possibility. Perspective reminds us that we are not victims of circumstance. Instead, we are active participants in shaping our lives. By choosing to look for the good, the opportunity, and the potential in every situation, we can create a life filled with purpose and meaning.

Chapter 21: Uncovering the True Self

The profound journeys a person can undertake for Self-discovery as It's not a destination that can be reached overnight, but a lifelong exploration of who we truly are, what drives us, and how we can grow. In a world filled with external pressures, distractions, and expectations, the path to understanding oneself often gets obscured.

The journey of self-discovery begins with weakness. To truly know yourself, you must be willing to face your fears, insecurities, and uncertainties. It requires a level of honesty that can sometimes feel uncomfortable, but it is only through this raw openness that you begin to strip away the layers of conditioning and discover what lies beneath. Vulnerability doesn't make us weak; it strengthens us by showing us where we need to grow.

One that unfolds with each step we take, each question we ask, and each layer we shed. It is through the process of becoming lost and found that we truly come to understand who we are. We often find ourselves living according to other people's definitions of success, happiness, and worth. To break free from this, you must question what truly matters to you. The only way to find out who you truly are is to listen to the quiet voice inside you that says, 'You are enough.' And then, take the next step into the unknown.

The beauty of self-discovery is that it's a lifelong journey. As we grow, change, and experience life, we constantly evolve. The person you are today is not the person you were a decade ago, and that's the essence of this path. It's a continuous process of learning, unlearning, and relearning. By embracing this journey, you step into a life of deeper meaning, connection, and fulfillment.

Chapter 22: The Power of Listening

Communication is more than just words; it's how we connect, understand, and share our worlds with each other. True communication is about more than talking, it's about listening, empathy, and creating spaces where people feel seen and heard.

It might seem simple, but real listening is a rare gift. To listen fully, without planning a response or assuming we know what the other person means, is a skill that builds trust and shows respect. People are more likely to engage when they feel understood and supported. When we listen to understand rather than to respond, we open up a bridge between ourselves and others.

Words hold power. They can encourage, inspire, and heal or they can hurt, divide, and disaffect. Speaking with intention means choosing words carefully and expressing yourself in a way that respects both your own feelings and those of others. It's not about perfect words, but genuine ones. Being mindful about what we say and how we say it can make even the most difficult conversations feel safe and respectful. When we speak with clarity and purpose, we allow others to understand us as we truly are. Much of our communication goes beyond words, through our body language, facial expressions, and even our silence. A simple smile, a nod, or steady eye contact can say more than words ever could. Paying attention to these silent cues helps us interpret the unsaid and convey support and understanding. Being aware of our non-verbal communication allows us to connect more deeply and shows others that we are fully present in the moment.

Not every conversation is easy, but difficult conversations often bring the most growth. Approach these situations with patience, respect, and openness helps transform potential conflicts into opportunities for better understanding.

Chapter 23: Creativity as a Lifelong Process

As we grow and change, so does our creativity. In childhood, creativity often manifests through curiosity and play, building imaginary worlds while playing with over love ones, solving puzzles makes us happy. As being adults, it emerges through our work where we deal with different things and the ways we face life's challenges. Each stage of life invites us to engage creatively, whether through pursuing a hobby, finding innovative solutions to problems, or developing unique perspectives in our career. Creativity isn't bound by skill level but by our willingness to engage our curiosity and stretch our thinking beyond the familiar.

keeping creative activities is a way to keep our brains active, be open to new things and sustain our curiosity. Life-long researches have shown that people who involve in creative activities throughout their life enjoy better mental strength and emotional health. Detracting from the challenges, turn to the creativity. It enables one to re-frame a situation or a problem, make adjustment and learn and that is how it contributes towards effective learning and growth.

Creativity flourishes when we allow curiosity within us, open ourselves up to the possibilities of new experiences, and think outside the orthodox box. While developing a skill that can be branded as fixed, creativity is a skill that people of all ages therefore it is always developing as it will develop to fit the upbringing and circumstances and education of the person. Hence when we let our creative inclination flow, we allow for and practice, self- evolution, and growth and we learn to cope with changes, as well as opportunities, in a new mature manner.

After all, creativity lies in the pleasure to learn and the ability to dream. It is one's ability to appreciate it, that will help people remain youthful and active in whatever they are engaging in. Be it in painting, working, or in relationships, creativity enhances the experience of life and every individual's realization of their potential.

Chapter 24: The Role of Emotions

Emotions are at the core of what it means to be human. They shape our experiences, drive our actions, and bring meaning to our lives. Whether it's joy, sadness, anger, or love, each emotion carries its own purpose, acting as a signal, guiding us in how we respond to the world around us. Emotions can be complex, sometimes overwhelming, but they're also what connect us deeply with ourselves and others.

Imagine life without emotions, it would feel hollow, lacking the highs and lows that make life vibrant and memorable. Joy lights up our happiest moments, while sadness teaches us about resilience and helps us appreciate brighter days. Even difficult emotions, like anger or fear, serve a purpose. Anger often highlights our values and boundaries, showing us what truly matters. Fear can protect us, sharpening our senses in the face of danger or pushing us to grow when we step outside our comfort zones.

Learning to understand and embrace our emotions gives us a fuller picture of who we are. Emotions aren't obstacles to overcome; they're part of our inner guidance system, signaling when something is right or wrong for us. The emotional brain responds to an event more quickly than the thinking brain.

Embracing emotions as a natural part of life allows us to lead with authenticity. They may not always be comfortable, but they make us human, adding depth and richness to our experiences. The role of emotions is not to be controlled or suppressed but to be acknowledged, learned from, and embraced as essential aspects of our journey.

Chapter 25: Magic of a Narrative

Storytelling is as old as humanity itself. It's how we've shared our knowledge, preserved our cultures, and made sense to the world. Whether through tales told around fires, stories written in books, or personal experiences shared with a friend, storytelling is a profound way we communicate, connect, and remember. Stories shape our beliefs, define our values, and often give us the courage to dream, feel, and imagine new possibilities. The power of storytelling lies not just in the words but in its ability to speak to our emotions, unite us through shared experiences, and leave a lasting impact.

At its heart, storytelling is how we pass down wisdom. For centuries, people have used stories to share lessons, inspire courage, and warn of dangers. In today's world, while the mediums have expanded to films, books, podcasts, and social media, the purpose remains the same: to communicate meaning and create connections. When we hear or read a story, we're invited into someone else's experience, expanding our own perspective and often discovering universal truths about life, love, fear, and joy.

The impact of storytelling on personal growth is also profound. Our personal stories are how we make sense of ourselves and our place in the world. When we share our experiences, we reveal parts of ourselves, making us vulnerable but also strengthening our connections with others. Telling our stories allows us to process our experiences and emotions, helping us heal, learn, and grow. Sometimes, the simple act of putting our thoughts into words can lead to breakthroughs, giving us clarity and empowering us to move forward. Listening to the stories of others can be equally transformative, offering us a sense of solidarity and understanding that we're not alone in our challenges.

Stories also have the unique ability to inspire change. Powerful narratives move us emotional, prompting us to think differently, see new possibilities, and sometimes even take action. Consider how films, books, and speeches have shaped movements for human rights, environmental preservation, and justice. Through storytelling, we can inspire others, spread empathy, and fuel positive change in the world.

On a more personal level, storytelling allows us to preserve memories and pass them down to future generations. Family stories, for example, keep our loved ones alive in our hearts, allowing us to honour and remember where we come from. These stories give us a sense of identity and continuity, connecting us to our past and grounding us in our values. They remind us of who we are and give us the strength to face the future, no matter what it may hold.

In essence, the power of storytelling is the power to connect. It bridges the gap between different generations, cultures, and experiences. Through storytelling, we share our joys, fears, and hopes, reminding us that while we may come from different backgrounds, our core experiences as human beings are remarkably similar. Every story, whether grand or small, adds something valuable to the world and has the potential to impact those who hear it.

Chapter 26: Time and Mortality

Understanding time as precious helps us prioritize what truly matters. When we think of time as a limited gift, it becomes easier to focus on what brings us joy and meaning. It encourages us to spend time wisely, Time is the most valuable thing a man can spend and pursue our dreams without delay. People always say time changes things, but you actually have to change them yourself.

Learning from mortality, we come to realize that facing life's end also brings a new beginning. Mortality teaches us to live with gratitude, to seek experiences that enrich our souls, and to let go of trivial worries that weigh us down. It is the acceptance of mortality that teaches us the importance of appreciating and being completely aware of – all moments and experiences. It is easier to love and allow forgiveness as well as connection. Because we wish to leave behind nothing but good in this world, as death gives birth to creative forces in us all. The realization about one's lifespan is both an invitation and a burden. It urges us not to put off dreams to love, to seek out reconciliation and most importantly, to act.

Live in the moment with a sense of proactivity and awareness since nothing lasts forever. Instead of dreading the conclusion, we can conceive of death as a sweet and dancing angel that urges us to respect and enjoy every single second, each and every person, and every opportunity that we come into contact with. Encounters with awareness of time its limits allow us to refuse unnecessary distractions and fill every single day with love and meaning, crafting a life that the soul will not be ashamed to remember.

Chapter 27: Wisdom in the Wrinkles

The wisdom of elders is a treasure passed down through generations a collection of lessons, stories, and insights that come only from a lifetime of experience. Elders have lived through cycles of change, faced countless challenges, and gained perspectives that only time and experience can offer. Their wisdom is a reminder of life's enduring truths, of values that stand the test of time, and of insights that help us navigate life's complexities with grace and resilience.

One of the greatest gifts elders offers is perspective. While youth is often driven by the immediacy of the present, elders encourage us to look beyond the immediate and understand the longer arc of life. They remind us that setbacks are temporary, that compassion is essential, and that love, kindness, and integrity are values that never fade. The wisdom they share can save us from repeating mistakes and open our eyes to life's deeper, often overlooked, meanings. Learning from elders connects us to our roots and gives us a sense of continuity and belonging. Their stories are threads that link us to a larger narrative, reminding us that we are part of something greater than ourselves. Their insights help us find direction and balance, guiding us toward a life that's not only successful by material standards but rich in purpose, character, and joy.

The wisdom of elders invites us to slow down, to listen, and to seek insight from those who have already walked the path. It teaches us to value life's lessons, to face adversity with resilience, and to approach others with compassion. By embracing the guidance of those who came before us, we gain not only wisdom but also a deeper connection to humanity, recognizing that we all have a role to play in preserving and passing on these invaluable lessons.

Chapter 28: Interconnected Web of Life

Imagine that all life on Earth is part of a single, vast web. In this web, every plant, animal, and person are like a thread woven into a larger, beautiful drapery. When we look closely, we see that no one part exists on its own each thread connects to another, supporting and shaping the whole. Understanding this helps us see that we are deeply connected to everything around us, bound together by our shared existence on this planet.

This web reminds us that even small actions can have big impacts. Just like a pebble dropped in a pond creates ripples, a single act of kindness or thoughtlessness spreads outward, affecting others and eventually finding its way back to us. The natural world shows us how this works. Think of bees pollinating flowers: by doing their small part, they help plants grow, providing food for countless other creatures. Humans are part of this same pattern. By caring for our environment, showing respect, and acting thoughtfully, we contribute to the health and harmony of the entire web.

At its heart, the interconnected web of life teaches us that we're never alone. The choices we make affect others, and the love and support we give to those around us ultimately come back to us, weaving a life filled with meaning and connection. In recognizing these ties, we see the importance of our actions, however small. We learn that life's richness comes from contributing to something larger than ourselves, honoring our connections with people, animals, and nature. It's a reminder that we're part of a shared journey, one that invites us to live with care, compassion, and respect for every living thing.

Chapter 29: Embracing Uncertainty

Uncertainty can make people rather uncomfortable, almost like walking into a dark room without an idea of which direction to follow. However, is also a certain reality of existence between the dangers that may happen and the wonders that may rise. Accepting the uncertainties of life in particular implies accepting the fact that many questions do not have answers, realizing that sometimes courage is all that is available in the face of the unknown and accepting that there are things that cannot be controlled, only experienced. If every one of us stops relating uncertainty to fear and instead sees it as a call to adjust, learn and discover, we will be able to make the best out of our lives. This means that one has a deeper understanding of uncertainty in the context of life. It means we learn to live with uncertainty about having clear next steps and answers for everything. This is not about avoiding the problems and difficulties but rather the resolution of the issue is very active and constructive. In this way, instead of closing off to the unknown, there is an attitude of interest where the unknown is only the avenue to anticipate that certain good outcome will happen, regardless of the prior attempts to plan things out rationally, and the feeling of satisfaction comes when it finally appears, although difference is that it has no regard of the plans.

Life is full of twists and turns we can't predict, and that's part of what makes it so rich and meaningful. By accepting uncertainty as an essential part of our journey, we learn to be brave, adaptable, and open to new possibilities. Embracing uncertainty encourages us to trust ourselves and the journey we're on, reminding us that life doesn't need to be entirely mapped out to be fully lived. Lastly there is no such thing as certainty. It's only an illusion that we create to ease our minds.

Chapter 30: The Gifts of Gratitude

Gratitude is often thought of as simply saying "thank you" or acknowledging the good things in life. But in reality, it's a much deeper practice, one that can transform the way we experience life. Gratitude doesn't just happen when everything is going well; it's a skill we can develop to find joy and contentment even in difficult moments. It unlocks the fullness of life. It turns what we have into enough, and more. It turns denial into acceptance, chaos to order, confusion to clarity. It can turn a meal into a feast, a house into a home, a stranger into a friend.

One interesting fact about gratitude is that it has a measurable impact on our mental and physical health. Studies show that people who regularly practice gratitude report higher levels of happiness, reduced stress, and even improved physical health. In one study, participants who wrote down things they were grateful for each day experienced fewer physical symptoms like headaches, compared to those who didn't practice gratitude. Other research found that gratitude improves sleep quality and can increase optimism by helping us focus on what we have rather than what we lack. Essentially, practicing gratitude reshapes our brain to notice and appreciate the positives, creating a boost to our well-being.

Practicing gratitude also helps to strengthen our relationships. When we take time to appreciate the people around us, we tend to become more empathetic, patient, and supportive. This can lead to stronger connections with friends, family, and even coworkers. Saying thank you to a friend for their support or showing appreciation for a loved one's kindness can deepen those relationships.

Another powerful aspect of gratitude is how it shifts our perspective. Instead of constantly focusing on what's missing or what we wish were different, gratitude encourages us to notice the small, everyday moments we often overlook. For example, a walk in the park on a sunny day, the sound of laughter, or a good conversation with a friend can be sources of happiness and fulfillment when viewed through the lens of gratitude. When we practice this regularly, life's challenges don't seem as overwhelming, and we're better equipped to face setbacks with resilience. Gratitude teaches us that, even in difficult times, there is something to appreciate and learn.

The practice of gratitude is a gift we can give ourselves daily. It reminds us that happiness isn't about waiting for perfect moments but about finding beauty and value in the journey itself. Through gratitude, we develop resilience, deepen our relationships, and build a more optimistic outlook on life. It's a powerful tool that reminds us of the richness already present in our lives, helping us to feel grounded, fulfilled, and at peace. Embracing gratitude opens our hearts to the abundance around us, turning ordinary days into extraordinary experiences.

Chapter 31: Creating a Shared Path

Building bridges starts with empathy, the ability to understand and share the feelings of another. When we make an effort to see the world from someone else's perspective, we begin to dissolve the barriers that often divide us. Empathy teaches us that, despite our differences, we share common human experiences like love, fear, joy, and sorrow. By actively listening to others and validating their experiences, we create a safe space for open dialogue. Over time, this kind of listening builds trust, fostering relationships that go beyond surface-level understanding.

Creating connections across differences also requires a willingness to embrace discomfort. Misunderstandings, awkward moments, or even conflict can arise when we engage with new perspectives. However, these challenges are essential to growth. Through honest conversations and a shared commitment to understanding, we can navigate these obstacles and find common ground. Each step we take toward understanding others strengthens the bonds between us, showing us that, ultimately, we are more alike than we are different.

Building bridges across differences allows us to expand our worldview and become better versions of ourselves. Each connection we make, each moment of understanding we share, enriches not only our lives but also the lives of those around us. Embracing diversity fosters unity, empathy, and respect, teaching us to appreciate the vast mosaic of humanity. Through this practice, we learn that the world is bigger, brighter, and more beautiful when we come together, hand in hand, across our differences.

Chapter 32: Mindfulness in Motion

In the hustle and bustle of modern life, it's easy to be swept away by distractions, obligations, and endless to-do lists. Our minds often wander to past regrets or future worries, making it challenging to experience the present moment fully.

Mindfulness is the art of paying attention, on purpose, without judgment. It's about noticing each experience as it comes, whether it's the taste of your morning coffee, the sound of birds outside, or the feeling of your breath moving in and out. When we practice mindfulness, we shift our focus away from the noise of past or future and root ourselves in the present. In this state, even ordinary moments become vivid and meaningful, as we learn to appreciate life as it unfolds rather than constantly rushing through it. Cultivating presence also helps us respond to life's challenges more thoughtfully. Instead of reacting impulsively, mindfulness allows us to take a step back, observe our emotions, and choose our responses intentionally. This simple pause can change everything, reducing stress and fostering greater resilience in difficult situations. For instance, when we encounter conflict or stress, being present allows us to stay calm, grounded, and open to solutions rather than feeling overwhelmed.

Embracing each moment, just as it is, invites more joy, peace, and authenticity into our lives, teaching us that the beauty of life lies in the small, quiet moments that are easy to overlook. Through presence, we discover that life's richness is always within reach right here, in the now.

Chapter 33: Healing Through Acceptance

The practice of forgiveness is our most important contribution to the healing of the world. It is not the burden of the past that harms us, but the refusal to let it go. In this chapter, we explore what it means to heal from life's inevitable wounds and how to reclaim our inner wholeness, understanding that these paths often intertwine.

Healing is not a linear process but a journey that ebbs and flows. It involves facing our deepest hurts, acknowledging our pain, and moving through it with patience and compassion. Often, we carry burdens from past experiences, memories, regrets, or fears that shape how we see ourselves and the world. You may not control all the events that happen to you, but you can decide not to be reduced by them.

Wholeness, on the other hand, is a return to our true selves a state where we embrace every part of who we are, including our imperfections and scars. It is not about reaching perfection but finding acceptance with all facets of ourselves. Wholeness teaches us that we are complete as we are, even in our brokenness. When we strive for wholeness, we let go of self-judgment and create space for kindness and forgiveness.

Healing and wholeness call us to self-reflect, to care for our scars and to acknowledge the beauty in how far we have come. It is a process that reminds us how it is not the goal of wellness to be flawless but rather complete. There is strength in healing; there is serenity in the state of being whole. The balance between the two provides a comforting reminder that we are strong and deserving of a happy and true existence irrespective of the circumstances.

Chapter 34: Adapting with Grace

Touching everything from our relationships and careers to our personal beliefs and habits. In our fast-paced world, change can feel overwhelming, but developing the skill to navigate it and to adapt can make a profound difference in our well-being and success.

Change, by nature, is often unpredictable and can arise suddenly. Psychologists estimate that adapting to change is one of the most important skills for personal resilience, helping us handle everything from minor disruptions to life-altering events. The human brain is wired to resist change as a survival mechanism; it finds comfort in familiar patterns and routines, which provide a sense of security. This resistance is often why we feel anxious or stressed when facing significant transitions. However, when we learn to reframe change as an opportunity rather than a threat, we can transform our experience. For example, a career shift, though initially daunting, can open doors to personal growth and discovery. It's not uncommon for people to find new passions or strengths during times of change, often looking back to realize that an unexpected turn led to some of their most fulfilling experiences.

Being adaptable doesn't mean ignoring feelings of fear or discomfort; rather, it's about acknowledging these emotions and moving forward despite them. In fact, embracing adaptability can foster a sense of personal empowerment, reminding us that we are not passive victims of change but active participants in shaping our lives. Adopting this mindset, we come to see change as an opportunity to learn, and grow.

Navigating change and building adaptability teach us that life's uncertainties are not roadblocks but pathways. As we learn to accept and even embrace the unknown, we find the courage to explore new possibilities and to let go of what no longer serves us.

Chapter 35: Alchemy of Transformation

Change is a fascinating concept; one that each and every individual has the ability to undergo. It is not just about putting on a new coat, but it is about the transformation which goes deep within changing an individual's very essence, bringing out the latent capabilities and exposing the real self. In this section, we will look at transformation and its magic of turning the positive and negative aspects of life into development, better understanding of oneself and fortitude.

Imagine that a person is being transformed. This usually starts from a small flicker. The flicker, almost always is ignited by a certain event in one's life. An event which challenges one's status quo or a conducive zone. For instance, sometimes it could be losing a certain standard or a way of life, getting adjusting with people surrounding you, or having the guts to pursue that passion made up in one's mind for years. Even though such experiences can be uncomfortable, they are likely to turn out to be radical, striving us towards at least a little good and deeper 'who am I' apart from this usual being and everyday routines. There is no transformation without learning that the discomfort is not something that is bad and should be evaded, but growth in disguise.

The power of alchemy lies in the fact that the process of change is not about evolving to be another person, but rather appreciating the need to change all facets of a person's life. When one applies this principle, it's similar to being gold and having oneself refined in the fire. One will throw away the things that do not fit them anymore- old fears, limiting beliefs, and life patterns that are counterproductive. This is not the most pleasant of journeys, but it is the most beautiful one, where one sheds out the old self and embraces a new self with no shame; vibrant and real.

Chapter 36: Awakening to Interbeing

Interbeing is the understanding that every single being on Mother Earth is connected, and that any action we partake makes an impact, not only on oneself but also on everyone and everything else. It is a notion that asks of us to step outside of the self to the appreciation of the fact that existence is not only dependent on the individual. In this section, we seek to investigate what acceptance of this relation means and how it makes us live.

Interbeing is a gentle reminder that we are all part of an interconnected whole, a shared world where each action we take has an impact beyond what we may realize. This awareness shifts our view of life from focusing solely on ourselves to recognizing our deep connection with others, the environment, and even the smallest elements of nature. Living with this understanding encourages us to act in ways that uplift, support, and protect the world around us.

Consider, for instance, how interconnected we are with nature. Trees produce the oxygen we breathe, while rivers, lakes, and oceans sustain the water we drink. Each element exists in a delicate balance, and when one part of this balance is disrupted, the effects can ripple throughout entire ecosystems. This interdependence can be humbling, showing us that each of us, while unique, is also part of a larger, shared ecosystem. Awakening to interbeing means appreciating this connection and acting with greater mindfulness toward the environment, recognizing that our actions today will shape the future we leave behind.

Most of the time we regard ourselves as individuals, detached from everyone except for ourselves, with personal objectives and ambitions. But when we begin to comprehend notions of interbeing and interconnectedness, we begin to realize that every one of us owes it to others as to why we eat what we eat, and leave what we leave.

We eat the food that farmers helped produce, the land and water nurtured; the things we use are produced by people in different countries. It dawns on us that we are in a more extensive world where we are enabled by many that we may not know or have a knowledge of.

To awaken to interbeing is to see life as a continuous, shared journey, where every action, thought, and choice has significance. It's an invitation to live more mindfully, to appreciate the connections that sustain us, and to contribute positively to a world that is truly, profoundly interconnected.

The realization of our interdependence brings with it an awareness of responsibility. With this understanding we become more concerned for the welfare of people and other beings around us as well as that of the environment in which we all exist. When we treat one another well, and treat one another with dignity, we are not only assisting people in our vicinity, but also making the world a bit more warm and friendly. This kind of awareness may be quite easy to practice, e.g., it could involve purchasing food from nearby growers, lessening consumption of resources, or simply stopping to consider all the individuals and all the activities that make our everyday life possible.

Finally, inter being teaches that it doesn't matter how small any of the activity seems, it can be of meaningful help when done in the right way. Letting in this way of life, fills us with appreciation, compassion, and purpose as we are patriotically aware of our small yet crucial role in this collective.

Chapter 37: Call to Contribute

The path of service is about finding ways to make a positive impact on the world, no matter how big or small. It's the idea that when we contribute to something beyond ourselves, we grow in meaningful ways. Living a life of service doesn't have to mean grand gestures; it often begins with simple acts of kindness or perhaps never gives beggar with the intention that we need more from God, as you are the real beggar.

Studies show that helping others not only benefits those we provide but also improves our well-being. Service brings a sense of fulfilment and purpose, as we realize that our actions can make a real difference. Whether it's through volunteering, supporting our local community, or simply being there for friends and family, contributing to others strengthens our sense of connection and purpose. Every person has something valuable to offer, and when we align our actions with a desire to serve, we become part of a larger, positive impact.

Living a life of service and contribution reminds us that we're part of a bigger picture. Each act, no matter how small, adds to the collective good and leaves a legacy of kindness and compassion. It's a reminder that we all have the power to uplift others and, in turn, to help create a world that's kinder, more inclusive, and more hopeful. The purpose of life is not to be happy. It is to be useful, to be honorable, to be compassionate, to have it make some difference that you have lived and lived well.

Chapter 38: The Sacredness of Life

Life itself is an incredible, mysterious gift a chance to experience, learn, grow, and connect in ways that can feel almost sacred when we pause to notice. The sacredness of life is an understanding that every moment, every being, every breath has intrinsic value.

At its core, seeing life as sacred is about respecting all living things recognizing that every person, plant, and creature has a unique role in the delicate balance of our world. Indigenous cultures around the world have long embraced this perspective, seeing nature not as a resource to exploit but as a living partner deserving of respect and care. Science, too, has uncovered just how interconnected life is. Each of us is composed of millions of cells working together in perfect harmony, an intricate system of intelligence that sustains us without our even realizing it. When we begin to see life this way, we come to honor it in the small and big moments alike.

This sacred view of life encourages us to approach every interaction, every choice, with intention. In seeing the beauty in others, we become more compassionate, understanding that each person carries their own unique story and struggles. To embrace the sacredness of life is to live more fully awake to the wonder that surrounds us. It means walking gently on the Earth, cherishing every sunrise, and every smile.

When we hold life as sacred, our lives naturally align with gratitude and reverence, and we cultivate a world where kindness, respect, and wonder become our guiding values.

Chapter 39: Art of Letting Go

One of the hardest and more profound lessons to accept about life is that of letting go. Whether it's releasing a cherished relationship, a long-held dream, or a sense of who we thought we were, the process of letting go can feel raw and vulnerable. But in that vulnerability lies the beauty of growth, a quiet strength that frees us to embrace new possibilities and new paths.

When we let go, we're not discarding or diminishing what once mattered to us. Instead, we're choosing to release its hold on our hearts, making space for healing and new discoveries. Some of us think holding on makes us strong, but sometimes it is letting go. To let go is not to forget, not to think about, or ignore. It is not to regret. Letting go is to trust. It is the acceptance of what is, and the courage to live without attachment.

Detachment from persons, places or things is a beautiful lesson taught in impertinence. Every interaction, moment and which and every experience for what they are, rather than wishing for what could have been. It enables us to turn loss into liberty, suffering into strength, and finishes into the start of something different. You don't need to know where you're going, you just need to know where you've been, and let go of it.

The more you let go, the less the weight of the world is on your shoulders. We find the quiet strength to move forward without the weight of expectations or the pull of the past, opening our hearts to new possibilities.

Chapter 40: Inspired by the Impossible

The impossible can feel like an unmovable mountain, but in every great endeavor, it's often the impossible that drives us to discover what we're truly capable of. Humanity has always been captivated by the challenge of the impossible, from reaching the stars to exploring the depths of our oceans. When we let the impossible inspire rather than intimidate us, we unlock a potential within ourselves that can achieve remarkable things.

This chapter is not only concerned with achieving greatness but also to explore how each of us has a battle to win; a battle where we each find courage within our personal mountains. We are, after all, moved by a cause greater than ourselves when we find the impossible, inspiring. It is not about ranting at naysayers or outperforming others; it is about finding out what we are capable of if we dream extremely and act on it. At these times, there is no fear or doubt that paralyzes us; only a strong conviction in what should we come to be and while we chase the impossible, we motivate those around us to do the same, thus all of us embark on a quest to a life without limits.

Being inspired by the impossible means believing that our greatest potential lies just beyond the obstacles we perceive. It challenges us to look inward, to cultivate resilience and creativity, and to meet life with a curiosity and wonder that makes the journey itself worthwhile. At last, what lies behind us and what lies before us are tiny matters compared to what lies within us.

Chapter 41: A World Created by Humans

We achieved many things as humans like cities rise from deserts, and digital networks span the globe, allowing us to connect instantly across oceans. Numerous numbers of things were invented to ease the lives of people living on earth. As we've built a society where growth, efficiency, and reaching towards something that once seemed impossible. Perhaps we've also identified some consequences that now call for solutions.

One of the realities is that we impacted nature poorly that cannot be healed as nature is unsettling its regular cycles. Air and water pollution compromise health, while climate change brings unpredictable weather and natural disasters. This world, as much as it reflects human brilliance, also mirrors the complexity of our choices. Humans prefer to enjoy things that are harmful for them, even if they know about them. The more you understand the things, the more you think why? I have understood that. Privacy has become a concern, as we already discussed before in the early chapter. Our technological advancements have brought ease and accessibility, yet they've also introduced new challenges. We've created our own creator, besides forgetting who had created all of us. It's sad that we value things as per fashion or things that influence us instead of what is right. Education on these issues must become a priority, helping individuals understand their role to reshape the world.

By aligning our advancements with respect for nature and each other, we can strive to leave a heritage that reflects not only our abilities but our values. Make our decision wisely. After all, nothing you will get by hating ourselves or others, as the most important lesson is to improve.

Chapter 42: Canvas of Forgiveness

Forgiveness is an art form, a blank canvas that allows us to rewrite stories marked by pain, loss, or betrayal. It is a bridge between past wounds and future peace, an act of courage that invites us to step away from resentment and step toward wholeness. Forgiveness is giving up the hope that the past could have been any different. A question arise that why should I forgive? Because the weak are incapable of forgiving, and a wise is recognized for forgiving others, rather than becoming spiteful. At its heart, forgiveness isn't about condoning harm or forgetting what happened; it's about choosing to no longer let that pain define us. To forgive is to reclaim our lives from the shadows of resentment and regret.

The ability to forgive is not limited to one's personal space; it is a healing tradition that knows no culture, society or age. It is important in a world full of disparities capable of causing deep misunderstandings that would last generations between people, communities or even nations. When we practice forgiveness, we learn to see one another as fellow human beings rather than as adversaries. It's a reminder that, regardless of our differences, we share the same desires for understanding, acceptance, and healing. In this way, forgiveness acts as a social balm, easing tensions and fostering empathy in a world that desperately needs it.

Self-forgiveness is equally essential but often overlooked. Many of us carry heavy burdens from past mistakes, harboring guilt or regret that clouds our ability to feel worthy of happiness. Forgiving ourselves is a radical act of kindness, an acknowledgment that we are all imperfect and that our missteps are opportunities to learn, grow, and become better versions of ourselves. Darkness cannot drive out darkness; only light can do that. Hate cannot drive out hate; only love can do that.

Chapter 43: Patterns of the Cosmos

The cosmos is a breathtaking wonder, filled with repeating patterns that feel like nature's rhythm, guiding life from the smallest cells to the grandest galaxies. Stars are born, live out their bright lives, and then release their energy back into space, seeding new stars and planets, a process that feels strangely familiar. Just as the universe keeps renewing itself, so do we, constantly growing and changing through the cycles of our lives.

In looking up at the stars, we can find comfort in the simple, repeating rhythms of nature: the orbits of planets, the phases of the moon, and the flow of tides. These cosmic patterns reflect the ups and downs we all face, showing us that life is made of cycles. Every change and challenge, each high and low, are part of a larger flow. When we recognize this, we begin to feel less lost in our own struggles, seeing that even our most difficult moments have a place in the big picture. The vastness of space, with its stars and galaxies stretching far beyond what we can see, humbles us, reminding us of our small yet meaningful place in the universe. We are the only beings, as far as we know, with the awareness to marvel at the cosmos and our place in it.

Thinking about the cosmos is a way to find balance in our own lives. We, too, are shaped by cycles and patterns, just as the stars are. The repeating beauty of the universe invites us to look for that harmony in ourselves. So, while we are tiny parts of an enormous whole, we're also extraordinary, carrying within us the ability to reflect on our place in this vast and incredible tapestry of life.

Chapter 44: A Journey to Harmony

Within each of us lies a blend of masculine and feminine energies. These are not about gender but rather two complementary forces that shape our lives. The masculine often represents action, logic, and structure, while the feminine embodies intuition, creativity, and nurturing.

When these energies are out of balance, life feels off-center. A focus on the masculine alone might lead to rigidity or burnout, while leaning too heavily into the feminine might bring a sense of being adrift without direction. But when these energies work together, they create harmony like a partnership where strength meets sensitivity, and drive is guided by care. Nature reflects this balance beautifully. Think of a river flowing freely, representing feminine energy, yet it needs the solid banks of masculine energy to give it direction and purpose. Both are essential, working together to create something life-giving and whole.

In our personal lives, this balance helps us grow. It allows men to show vulnerability and kindness without fear, and it encourages women to stand in their strength and independence with confidence. Beyond ourselves, this harmony fosters understanding in relationships, workplaces, and communities, creating spaces where everyone feels seen and valued.

Balancing these energies is not about choosing one over the other but recognizing their equal importance. It's a journey of self-awareness, of embracing all parts of ourselves and respecting the same in others. When we find this balance, life feels more aligned, more peaceful, and more connected. It's a reminder that strength and softness, action and reflection, belong together and together, they create something truly beautiful with this world.

Chapter 45: The Essence of Being Human

At our core, we are more than the roles we play, the titles we hold, or the identities we wear. The essence of us, the part that defines who we truly are? is something deeper, something timeless. It is the quiet presence that connects us to life itself, the part of us that feels love, dreams of possibilities, and seeks meaning beyond the ordinary.

This essence is what unites us as human beings, reminding us that beneath our differences in culture, beliefs, or experiences, we share something universal. It's the thread that weaves humanity together, the capacity to care, to create, to hope, and to endure. Even in moments of struggle, the essence of us is what rises to meet challenges with resilience and grace.

But in the rush of daily life, we often forget to listen to this inner voice. We become tangled in distractions, chasing external validation or material success, and lose sight of what truly matters. Yet, the essence of us is always there, waiting quietly, like the stillness beneath a storm, guiding us back to what feels real and true.

Discovering and honoring this essence doesn't require grand gestures. It's found in the small, quiet moments: the warmth of a genuine smile, the peace of watching a sunset, the joy of creating something meaningful, or the connection in simply being present with someone else. These moments remind us of who we are and what makes life worth living.

Chapter 46: Aligned Resonance

It's about moving through life in a way that feels genuine, natural, and connected. When we achieve this alignment, life flows more easily, with less resistance and more joy.

Resonance is the feeling of being in sync with something greater than yourself. It's that moment when you feel completely present, where your actions reflect your purpose, and where your choices uplift both yourself and others. Alignment, on the other hand, is the structure that makes this resonance possible. It's the clarity to know what truly matters to you and the courage to live according to those values, even when it's challenging.

But how do we embody resonance and alignment in our lives? It starts with awareness, an honest look at what energizes you and what drains you. When you listen to your inner compass, you begin to notice where you feel at home and where you feel out of place. From there, it's about taking small, consistent steps toward what feels right, even if it means letting go of what no longer serves you. This isn't always easy. Society often pulls us in directions that may not align with our true selves like chasing success, conforming to expectations, or silencing our intuition. But when we trust our inner guidance, we find a path that feels more authentic and fulfilling. Living in resonance doesn't mean life will always be smooth, but it does mean you'll face challenges with a sense of purpose and confidence.

It's not about perfection but about integrity: the ability to align your choices with your heart and mind. When you live this way, you create a ripple effect, inspiring others to do the same.

Chapter 47: Woven in Chaos

We humans always think very much about life and can't help with that because creation and destruction thread together to shape this earth.

From stars exploding to create new galaxies to ancient civilizations rising and falling, this dance is constant and unstoppable. It's neither good nor bad, it simply is. To live fully, we must embrace this chaos as part of the journey. Creation is the spark of life, the birth of a child, the dawn of an idea, or the start of a new chapter. It's filled with hope, possibility, and the thrill of what could be. But every act of creation emerges from something that came before. Every act of creation is first an act of destruction.

Destruction, though often painful, is not just an end, it's the beginning of something new. Forest fires, while devastating, prepare the soil for fresh growth. A breakup, though heartbreaking, can lead to personal transformation. In chaos, we find renewal. Life is about change and nothing ever stands still.

The balance between creating and letting go is what keeps life moving forward. Imagine a painter reworking their canvas, each stroke, an adjustment, each erased line, a chance to refine. Similarly, in our lives, letting go of old habits, fears, or grudges makes room for something better. This cycle of chaos is what teaches us resilience and adaptability. It reminds us that endings are not failures but doorways, and beginnings hold untold potential. Chaos may seem overwhelming, but it is also the force that drives growth and transformation.

In the fabric of our lives, we hold the power to weave with intention. Life invites us to find harmony within its woven patterns, shaping something beautiful even in the storm.

Chapter 48: The Infinite Beyond

What if every choice you made created a new reality? What if there were countless versions of you, living out alternate paths? These ideas aren't just the stuff of science fiction, they are serious questions being explored in modern science and philosophy. The concept of the multiverse, where parallel realities exist simultaneously, opens a world of wonder and reflection.

The multiverse theory suggests that our universe is just one of many. Each universe may have its own laws of physics, timelines, and possibilities. Imagine a version of you who pursued a different career, or another where you made that leap you were too scared to take. Everything is connected with universe we are living in. It's humbling to think we might only be one thread in a vast cosmic tapestry. But it's also empowering. If infinite realities exist, the life we choose to live here and now matters all the more. Our decisions carry weight in shaping the reality we experience.

The multiverse also inspires us to think beyond the limits of what we know. It challenges us to imagine what's possible, to dream bigger, and to embrace the mystery of existence. Somewhere, something incredible is waiting to be known.

While we may never fully grasp the true nature of the multiverse, exploring the idea expands our understanding of reality. It invites us to question what's real, what's possible, and how our lives fit into the grander picture. Perhaps the greatest truth of all is this: whether there's one universe or many, the magic lies in how we choose to live within it.

Chapter 49: Faith in Flow

In a world that often glorifies control, the path of devotion and surrender offers a profound counterbalance. It is not about giving up or losing oneself but about opening the heart to something greater or the mystery of life itself.

Devotion is a deep, unwavering commitment to what truly matters. Surrender, often misunderstood as weakness, is actually an act of courage. Try not to resist the changes that come your way. Instead, let life live through you. And do not worry that your life is turning upside down. How do you know that the side you are used to is better than the one to come?

This path teaches us humility and openness. By surrendering to life's ebbs and flows, we connect more deeply with ourselves and others. It allows us to experience the profound joy of living in harmony with the world rather than fighting against it.

Walking the path of devotion and surrender doesn't mean abandoning responsibility or ambition. It means aligning our actions with our deepest values and trusting the process. It's about understanding that while we may not control every outcome, we can control how we show up with love, presence, and faith.

In surrender, we find peace. In devotion, we find purpose. Together, they create a life that feels full and meaningful, even amidst challenges. This path reminds us that the journey is not just about reaching a destination but about how we walk along the way, guided by the light of our hearts.

Chapter 50: Parenting with Presence

Parenting is one of life's most profound and transformative experiences. It is a journey not just of raising a child but of nurturing their essence while growing alongside them. Conscious parenting invites us to approach this role with awareness, empathy, and intentionality, fostering not only the child's growth but also our own.

At its heart, conscious parenting is about seeing the child as an individual, not as an extension of ourselves or as a project to be perfected. It's about embracing their unique strengths, emotions, and challenges with patience and love. Instead of controlling or molding them, conscious parenting encourages guiding and supporting them as they discover their path.

Often, children mirror back our unhealed wounds, fears, and insecurities. By reflecting on these triggers and working to heal them, parents can break cycles of generational patterns and create healthier dynamics. Children are educated by what the grown-up is and not by his talk. It emphasizes active listening, validating feelings, and understanding the child's perspective. Discipline, in this context, becomes less about punishment and more about teaching and nurturing emotional intelligence. This approach builds trust, resilience, and a secure bond that lays the foundation for lifelong relationships.

In a fast-paced, achievement-driven world, conscious parenting calls us to slow down and prioritize presence. Whether it's sharing a quiet moment, engaging in meaningful play, or simply being there without distractions, these acts of presence convey love more deeply than words ever could.

Chapter 51: Unwritten Chapters of Hope

Hope is the thread that connects us to the infinite possibilities of tomorrow. It is the quiet yet unyielding belief that no matter how dark the night, dawn is always within reach.

This chapter tell us to explore the power of hope as a guiding force. It is not blind optimism or ignoring the difficulties we face but rather the courage to envision a better future and take steps toward it. Isn't it when we are no longer able to change a situation, we are challenged to change ourselves. In our personal lives, hope is the seed of transformation. It is what propels someone to keep striving for love after heartbreak, to rebuild after failure, or to heal after pain. These unwritten chapters are where resilience is born, where we rewrite the narrative of defeat into one of perseverance and triumph.

On a collective level, hope is the foundation of progress. Every great achievement in human history began with someone daring to believe in what others deemed impossible. Hope fuels innovation, ignites movements for change, and bridges divides between people and nations. It is the unseen energy behind every act of kindness, every step toward justice, and every effort to heal our planet.

But hope is not a passive force. It demands action. Writing the unwritten chapters of hope means stepping into the unknown with faith, making choices that align with the future we want to create, and inspiring others to do the same. It means planting seeds of kindness even when the soil seems barren, standing up for what is right even when it feels like no one is listening, and believing in humanity's capacity to grow and learn.

In the book of life, hope is the ink with which we write. Let us use it generously and bravely, knowing that every word we pen shapes the world we leave behind. Hope is the thing with feathers that perches in the soul and sings the tunes without the words and never stops at all.

Hope also teaches us the value of patience. Just as a seed must rest in the soil before it can bloom, the fruits of hope often take time to reveal themselves. It may not always provide immediate results, but it holds the promise of growth and renewal. When we nurture hope, even in the smallest ways, we create ripples that can eventually transform entire oceans.

Hope isn't confined to grand, heroic acts. It is found in the quiet moments of everyday life, in a teacher encouraging a struggling student, in a doctor who doesn't give up on a challenging case, in a parent who sacrifices to ensure a better future for their child. These are the stories of unsung heroes who write the unwritten chapters every single day. Out of suffering have emerged the strongest souls; the most massive characters are seared with scars.

The unwritten chapters of hope are also deeply personal. They remind us that each of us carries within us the power to rewrite our own stories. Whether we're facing personal struggles or global challenges, hope gives us the courage to turn the page and begin again. It's the quiet voice that says, "Keep going," even when the world feels heavy.

Chapter 52: Mysteries of the Mind

We hold many things in our mind as human mind is an enigma of thoughts, dreams, and emotions. It's the source of our creativity, the keeper of our memories, and the driver of our deepest fears and desires. It holds the power to create worlds, conjure dreams, and unravel the deepest puzzles of existence. What lies beneath the surface of our thoughts? What fuels our emotions? The conscious mind is the part we know best. It's the voice in our head, the logical reasoning that helps us navigate daily life.

The mind is its own place and, in itself, can make a heaven of hell, a hell of heaven. The way we think about our experiences, challenges, and triumphs defines how we live. A single thought can spark joy, while another can drown us in doubt.

Our minds are also the architects of perception. What we see, hear, and feel isn't just reality, it's our brain's interpretation of it. Two people can witness the same event and remember it entirely differently, shaped by their biases, emotions, and past experiences. This is why perspective matters so deeply. When we open our minds to see beyond our narrow view, we unlock a broader, richer understanding of the world.

But the mysteries of the mind aren't just abstract, they're deeply personal. Have you ever wondered why certain thoughts linger, no matter how hard you try to push them away? Or why your mind sometimes feels like a battlefield, filled with doubts and fears alongside hope and determination? Whether you think you can, or you think you can't, you're right as when we fill our minds with belief, courage, and positivity, we create paths to new possibilities. But when we allow fear and self-doubt to take over, we block our potential. By exploring the depths of our thoughts and emotions, we uncover not just who we are, but who we can become.

Chapter 53: Generational Ties

Every generation is like a thread in the vast tapestry of human existence, woven together to tell the story of where we've been and where we're going. From the wisdom of elders to the energy of youth, each generation offers something invaluable, bridging the past, present, and future. But how often do we pause to appreciate these connections and understand their significance?

The bond between generations is more than just a passing of time, it's the transfer of values, knowledge, and dreams. Think of the stories shared by grandparents, tales of struggles, love and loss. These narratives become the foundation of our identity, grounding us in a legacy that is greater than ourselves. We are the ancestors of tomorrow, weaving the lessons of yesterday into the hopes of today.

Yet, the connection isn't without its challenges. Each generation is shaped by its own set of circumstances, sometimes these differences can create gaps in understanding. The older generation may view the younger as impulsive or detached, while the younger may see the older as resistant to change. But within these differences lies an opportunity: the chance to bridge the gap through empathy, and mutual respect.

In today's world, technology plays a crucial role in connecting generations. A grandmother learning video calls to speak with her grandchildren on the other side of the world, or a young child listening to old records with their parents, are moments that highlight the beauty of shared experiences. But beyond technology, the heart of connection remains the same: the desire to feel seen, valued, and understood.

We acknowledge that we stand on the shoulders of those who came before us while paving the way for those who will follow. By fostering this bond, we ensure that wisdom is never lost, dreams are never forgotten, and humanity continues to thrive.

Chapter 54: The Way of the Heart

Heart is the symbol of everything that makes us human. It holds our capacity to love, forgive, feel joy, and endure pain.

The best and most beautiful things in the world cannot be seen or even touched, they must be felt with the heart. The way of the heart isn't always the easiest path; it demands a willingness to confront our fears. But it's the most rewarding, for it leads us to authenticity and true connection. Follow your heart, but take your brain with you.

On this path, the heart teaches us about the power of presence. To truly live is to savor each moment fully, to laugh deeply, cry openly, and love. It's not how much we give but how much love we put into giving.

Yet, the way of the heart is also about balance, loving others without losing yourself. It's about knowing when to let go and when to hold on. As you walk this path, remember that the heart's wisdom is always within you. When life feels overwhelming, listen closely and it often whispers where the mind shouts. Let its quiet guidance shape your actions and lead you toward a life of meaning.

We find the essence of humanity. It's in the love we give and the compassion we show. It's in the moments we share, the bonds we build, and the legacy of kindness we leave behind. Let this be the way we journey forward: with hearts wide open and spirits unyielding.

The heart speaks a language the mind often struggles to understand, its words are love, its rhythm is courage, and its purpose is connection. The heart is a compass that often points us toward truths the mind cannot comprehend. It speaks in the language of love, whispers courage in moments of doubt, and bridges the divide between connection and isolation. To live through the heart is to embrace a life of depth and authenticity, where every action, no matter how small, is infused with meaning.

Chapter 55: Purpose of Human Creation

What is the purpose behind the human design? Why are we here, equipped with minds that dream, hearts that feel, and hands that create? These questions have haunted and inspired humanity for generations. The answer lies not in the mechanics of our bodies but in the essence of our existence on what roles we play, the connections we forge, and the legacy we leave.

When we talk about purpose, we are not merely beings meant to survive; we are meant to thrive, to grow, and to make the world better than we found it. Unlike other creatures, we carry within us the capacity for imagination, a unique gift that allows us to envision realities beyond what exists. This ability gives us the responsibility to create meaning, solve problems, and shape futures.

Every person is a piece of the continent, a part of the main. Each role, no matter how small it may seem, contributes to the vast web of life. This design is not random it is intentional. We are built for interdependence, for shared growth, and for the collective evolution of our species.

We are created to learn from our experiences, adapt to challenges, and transform through adversity. Our mistakes are not failures but stepping stones, guiding us toward wisdom and clarity. With each step, we draw closer to understanding our unique place in the grand tapestry of existence. The universe is not outside of you. Look inside yourself; everything that you want, you already are. Everyone has been made for some particular work, and the desire for that work has been put in every heart.

Chapter 56: Influenced by Others

We live in a world where the smallest of interactions can leave the biggest impressions. Our words, actions, and behaviors ripple out like waves, touching the lives of others in ways we often cannot see. We are all mirrors to one another. When someone radiates positivity, it has the power to brighten even the darkest days. Conversely, negativity can pull us into shadows we didn't know existed. The reality is that influence doesn't require intention. It happens in every interaction, every shared moment, and every silent gaze. That's the reality of influence, it's happening all the time, whether we notice it or not.

We rise by lifting others. This isn't just a saying; it's a way of life. When we choose kindness, when we act with love, we're not only helping others, we're helping ourselves. People will forget what you said, people will forget what you did, but people will never forget how you made them feel.

The weight we caring of others and the unknown we won without letting them know. every one of us has the power to change someone's day, even their life, for better or worse. So why not choose to be the reason someone feels valued, understood, and inspired? I know that someone words can be hurtful as life is too short to be weighed down by the judgments of those who don't see your light but as the same time when someone believed in you like a friend who reminded how about your true potential or even a stranger who gave you a smile when you needed it most. That's what we can give to others, too. It's not about grand gestures. Often, it's the little things, a kind word, a helping hand, that make all the difference. The most important thing in this world is to let someone know they are loved.

Be intentional with your influence. Recognize the power in your words, gestures, and silence. In a world that sometimes feels chaotic, one kind act has the power to change the shape of a life.

Chapter 57: Stories in the Soil

The ground beneath us is more than a foundation for our steps, it is a vault of human history, cradling the stories of those who shaped the world with their choices and actions. Every grain of soil carries echoes of people who dared to dream, who persevered in the face of challenges, and whose lives were woven into the fabric of the earth.

These stories remind us that true impact is not measured by the grandeur of our achievements but by the depth of our contribution. From the hands that built communities to the hearts that inspired movements, every act, no matter how small, adds to the collective narrative of humanity. The soil carries these stories in silence, preserving the essence of resilience, vision, and hope. But the earth doesn't just carry tales of triumph. It bears witness to mistakes, to the scars of overuse and neglect, to times when humanity took more than it gave. These shadows are just as significant, for they teach us humility and the urgent need for change. The soil reminds us that we are temporary stewards, entrusted with preserving its richness for future generations.

Every moment, we stand on the history of those who came before us while shaping the foundation for those who will come after. It is a cycle of contribution of What will you leave behind? Will it nourish the world or burden it? The soil holds the whispers of the past and the seeds of the future. Let this be a reminder to act with intention, to walk with purpose, and to plant seeds.

Our footsteps today will become the stories of tomorrow. Let us tread lightly, live meaningfully, and create a legacy that not only honors the earth but enriches it for generations to come.

Chapter 58: The Shadow of Progress

Progress, often celebrated as humanity's crowning achievement. For every step forward, there's a shadow, a quiet cost we sometimes fail to acknowledge. What have we left behind in this rush toward the future? The question we must ask ourselves is not just how far can we go? but how wisely can we proceed?

True progress isn't measured by speed or scale; it is revealed in the quality of the journey and the impact left in its wake. Often, the world applauds those who shout the loudest, achieve the fastest, and conquer the most. But real growth, the kind that changes lives and nurtures the soul, happens in the quiet spaces, when no one is watching, when intentions are pure, and when actions align with a deeper purpose.

Silence is not the absence of progress; it is the root of its truth. Progress built on mindfulness, where quiet reflection shapes bold action, lasts longer and heals deeper. The ones who truly shape the world are often unseen, their work not marked by noise but by the strength of their principles. We need to learn to advance without trampling what is sacred, to grow without losing what is essential. Each of us plays a part in shaping this balance. When we act with intention, when we consider not just the next achievement but its legacy, we become the quiet builders of a brighter world. In the shadow of progress lies the wisdom to create a future that honors the past while embracing what's to come.

This is the silent art of building something meaningful, progress that doesn't seek recognition but leaves behind a world worth inheriting. Let us walk forward with purpose, knowing that true greatness grows not in the light of applause but in the shadow of thoughtful care.

Chapter 59: Ecology of Kindness

We have seen people become what they once laughed at, so always be humble. A smile, a kind word, or even just listening to someone when they need to talk, these moments matter more than we realize. Kindness doesn't just help others; it heals us, too. Think of kindness as planting seeds. You may not always see how those seeds grow, but they can blossom into something beautiful in someone's life. When you help a stranger, encourage a friend, or even show yourself a little compassion, you're adding to a world that's softer, gentler, and more connected.

Kindness is the language which the deaf can hear and the blind can see. We rise by lifting others. No act of kindness, no matter how small, is ever wasted. his simple truth reminds us that what seems insignificant can create powerful wave. Being kind also means being kind to yourself. We're often our harshest critics, carrying guilt, shame, or self-doubt. But when you treat yourself with understanding and forgiveness, you grow stronger inside. That strength allows you to be a better friend, partner, or parent. Kindness starts within, and from there, it spreads outward.

Kindness is not an act; it is a way of life. t's in how we choose to treat one another in everyday moments. It's the glue that holds relationships together and the spark that makes life meaningful.

In a world where you can be anything, be kind. When we choose kindness, we choose hope. And when enough of us make that choice, the world becomes a little brighter, one small act at a time, spread it freely, and watch it grow.

Chapter 60: Whisper of the Stars

The stars on the velvet canvas of the night, though mere glowing objects, are in reality ancient narrators of tales. Each flaunts its story of birth, metamorphosis, and resilience, which is reminiscent of life itself. Looking up into the vastness of stars reminds us of the language of the universe, light, which beckons the soul to listen rather than eyes or ears.

It is in the midst of stars that mankind has found the greatest of their questions. Who am I? Why am I here? What is beyond? They connect us to the infinite beyond the earthly influences. Stars remind us that while life can appear overwhelming, we belong to a greater narrative, one woven through patience and purpose. This is no more than the boon "the stars have borne witness to the perseverance of light over darkness." The true and simple truth is something we can carry in our hearts. No matter how awful the night may seem, the stars remain a small and quiet reminder that light will always make its way through.

It is hardly noisy and no longer than a whisper, unlike life itself: this is how the stars speak to us, teaching us about stillness and reflection. Ever-present but never overbearing, they ask for nothing but give everything-a hallmark of grandeur and humility. They teach us how to shine in humility, illuminating others without expectation.

When it is darkest, the stars appear the brightest. This makes us reflect on our lives. Trials and tribulations often open the realms of inner light, strength, and the potential for serving as an inspiration for others. And just as stars come about through cosmic chaos, it is from the crucible of adversity that some of the finest strengths emerge.

Chapter 61: The Courage to Pause

Indeed, some might consider that the pause means the movement is countering the revolutionized world. But it is a specific kind of daring- the daring that stays, ponders, and visualizes clearly what really counts- to rest. One does not withdraw something when one takes a step back but on the contrary, it gives you an edge when you are leaving. Sometimes the best one should do is to sleep. This is not a call to slothfulness but to tune oneself to nature's rhythms. The seasons follow their inter-changeable stoppages. Thus, we should, sometimes, give ourselves sack by stillness. The fortitude to stop means that you have come to terms with the fact that life is a continuum not a sprint and that moments are intentionally to be cherished.

Trees rest in winter and yet their roots sink deeper. Instead of running, pause, and get a close solution of inner strength that makes our deepest roots thrive underneath our life and passion. Silence nurtures the birth of clarity during a break. It's not in noise but in serene moments the heart has a voice. The ability to cut off the distracting surroundings prompts the silence of our hearts here. This is, the space that brings us closer to our truth, wisdom, and peace.

The world stretches a further veil on our faces for flight rather than reflection and more enjoyment than enjoyment. There are times you find it outdo or a retreat is intrinsic. The times of rest and meditation are the times that get us back to our hearts and allow us to revisit those wonders we glide by in a rush. The moon even halts before rising, thereby bestowing the stars their share of time. Pauses like these tell us that counting life isn't done by speed, but by depth.

To pause is to reclaim our power. It's an act of self-respect, a declaration that we are more than the sum of our accomplishments. The greatest battles are often won in the quiet moments of reflection.

Chapter 62: Living in the Threshold

Life is full of thresholds and those in-between spaces where the past and the future meet, and we find ourselves suspended in uncertainty. These moments, though often uncomfortable, are not just transitions but profound opportunities to grow, redefine, and embrace the unknown. To live in the threshold is to accept life's ever-changing nature, a lesson that demands courage, patience, and faith.

Thresholds are the places where life shifts between endings and beginnings, losses and discoveries, doubts and decisions. They are often unsettling because they lack clarity and certainty. Yet, they hold extraordinary power. It is in these spaces that we learn resilience. Out of chaos, stars are born. Thresholds remind us that while the road ahead may seem unclear, every step forward reveals new possibilities.

In these moments, we are called to face our fears. Fear of the unknown, fear of failure, or even fear of change itself can feel paralyzing. But thresholds demand that we step beyond these fears. You can only step into the future if you let go of the shore. Letting go is never easy, but it is essential to progress.

Living in the threshold also requires us to confront ourselves. Without the stability of our usual roles, we are left with raw questions: Who am I? What do I truly desire? These questions are uncomfortable, yet they pave the way for self-discovery. The journey isn't about becoming something else; it's about unbecoming everything that isn't you.

While thresholds are spaces of reflection, they are also ripe for imagination. When we stand in the doorway between what was and what could be, we are given the rare chance to dream without limits. In the gap between the old and the new lies the power to rewrite your story. Creativity flourishes in these moments of ambiguity because they free us from rigid expectations.

However, the threshold is not solely about action; it's also about stillness. It teaches us the art of presence, of being fully immersed in the here and now. In a world that constantly urges us to move, achieving this stillness can feel revolutionary. The quieter you become, the more you can hear.

Thresholds remind us that life is not linear. We often circle back, take detours, or pause altogether. And that's okay. These twists and turns are part of the process. The path may be unclear, but every step forward illuminates the next. Even when we feel lost, the act of moving, no matter how small, brings us closer to clarity.

Some of the most profound transformations occur in the threshold. It's the place where we learn to let go of what no longer serves us and to embrace what's waiting to unfold. The butterfly must struggle to leave the cocoon; it's the struggle that gives its wings the strength to fly.

Living in the threshold also calls for faith, faith in ourselves, faith in the process, and faith in the idea that life, in its mysterious way, always works out. "What is meant for you will not pass you by. This faith sustains us when the ground beneath us feels shaky and uncertain.

Finally, thresholds teach us gratitude. They show us that every moment of discomfort and doubt is a precursor to something beautiful. The strongest steel is forged in the hottest fire. We may not see the bigger picture immediately, but in hindsight, these transitions often become the most meaningful chapters of our lives.

So, let us embrace the thresholds, not as barriers but as gateways to growth. These are the spaces where we are reshaped, refined, and reborn. Every ending is a new beginning in disguise. In living through them, we discover not only who we are but who we are capable of becoming. And that, perhaps, is the most extraordinary journey of all.

Chapter 63: The Cross-Cultural Bond

As we know the world that grows are interconnected, while living here we humans made different types of cultures offering a unique blend of richness and challenges.

When two people from different cultures come together, they bring with them not just their personal stories but the weight of traditions, values, and histories. These differences can sometimes feel like barriers, but they also hold the key to profound learning. Every person you meet is a door to a new world. Relationships that navigate these cultural landscapes require an openness to explore those worlds without judgment or fear.

Communication is always a cornerstone of this concept where misunderstandings are inevitable when languages, idioms, or non-verbal cues differ, but these moments can also be opportunities. It's not about speaking the same language; it's about hearing the same heart. What we take for granted, be it traditions, family roles, or social norms and may be entirely different for someone else. Instead of clinging to the familiar, these differences encourage us to expand our horizons. Your world expands every time you step into someone else's shoes.

Food, festivals, art, and rituals often become mediums through which cultures merge. Sharing meals cooked from generations-old recipes or participating in celebrations foreign to one's upbringing fosters a sense of belonging and appreciation. Challenges will arise, especially when deeply ingrained beliefs collide. But these moments are where the real work of building bridges happens. Strength lies not in avoiding conflict, but in growing through it together. Listening with patience, valuing the other person's perspective, and finding a middle ground are acts of love that can fortify any relationship. Listening with patience, valuing the other person's perspective, and finding a middle ground are acts of love that can fortify any relationship.

At their core, cultural bridges in relationships teach us about unity. They remind us that differences are not meant to divide but to enrich. We are not the same, but that's what makes us stronger together. Love is not about erasing differences but weaving them into a shared story. In every culture, every story, and every heart lies the potential to build bridges that connect us, not just to each other but to the deeper truths of our shared humanity.

In these relationships, curiosity becomes our greatest ally. Asking questions like, "Why does this matter to you?" or "What does this mean in your culture?" opens doors to deeper understanding. It's not about knowing every tradition but about valuing the heart behind them. One of the most beautiful aspects of cultural bridges is the blending of traditions. A shared life may mean decorating for festivals from both cultures or merging customs to create new family rituals. These moments of harmony show us that cultures are not meant to compete but to complement. In every handshake of cultures lies a reminder that unity is not sameness but the celebration of difference.

There is also humility in these relationships, a willingness to admit when we don't know or when we get something wrong. It's okay to stumble over unfamiliar customs or make mistakes. What matters is the intention to learn and grow. It's not about perfection; it's about progress, about walking towards each other with open hearts. Love grows deepest where understanding takes root.

Ultimately, these relationships are reflections of the world we hope to create, one where differences are not barriers but stepping stones to something greater. They remind us that while we may come from different shores, we all belong to the same ocean of humanity.

Chapter 64: Realities of Marriage

Marriage is often painted as a fairytale with many ups and downs. An unending celebration of love, and companionship. But the truth is, marriage is much more profound. It is not just the merging of two lives but the intertwining of two souls, complete with their imperfections, fears, and dreams. The reality of marriage lies not in its grand moments but it's to choose your partner every day, to care, and to grow together.

Those who live happily in their married life often live longer than their unmarried or divorced counterparts. A stable marriage can promote physical and emotional well-being. At its core, marriage is about partnership. It's standing side by side, weathering life's storms and celebrating its sunny days. Challenges comes in everything conflicts arise, compromises are made, and patience is tested in everything. But these moments of struggle are not signs of failure, these are things to learn and experience your life to make it more beautiful. A strong marriage isn't built on the absence of conflict but on the presence of commitment.

In marriage, love evolves. What begins as passion matures into a deep sense of belonging and understanding. There are days of excitement and days of routine, but the beauty lies in finding meaning in the ordinary, shared meals, quiet evenings, or even silent moments of simply being together. True love is not about perfection; it's about finding joy in each other's imperfections.

Expressing needs, listening actively, and offering words of kindness and affirmation build bridges even in moments of disagreement. Marriage is not just about loving each other; it's about trusting the journey you're building together.

Chapter 65: Strength in Sacrifice

The one who most sacrifice never tell you. Sacrifice is one of life's quiet truths often misunderstood and overlooked. We think, why do we have to lose something? It's not about losing something; it's about giving something meaningful for a greater purpose. sacrifice is an act of love, courage, and hope. It's the parent working late hours to provide a better future for their children, the friend who puts their own needs aside to be there for someone in pain, or the dreamer who chooses hard work over comfort to chase something extraordinary.

True strength doesn't come from what we hold onto but from what we're brave enough to let go of. In a fast-paced world that glorifies success and self-interest, sacrifice reminds us of what truly matters. It's the silent hero in every great story. Think of a candle. As it burns, it gives its light to others, losing itself in the process but illuminating everything around it. Sacrifice works in much the same way. It may seem like we're losing something in the moment, but we're actually creating possibilities for others and ourselves. Sacrifice is not about pain; it's about purpose. It's about believing that what we give can create something bigger than ourselves.

Life often calls for sacrifices when we least expect it. It's not easy, but it's a choice that shapes our character. The moments when we put someone else's happiness above our own, or choose to work toward something without immediate rewards, are the moments when we grow the most. The truth is, sacrifice isn't weakness, it's strength in its purest form. It's the courage to prioritize love, kindness, and vision over ego and fear.

When we sacrifice with an open heart, the universe has a way of returning it in ways we never imagined. A single act of selflessness can inspire others, building a world rooted in compassion and understanding. It shows us that the most beautiful things in life such as trust and connection often come from what we're willing to give.

I care about something greater than myself, It's not a burden but a choice. In every act of sacrifice lies a silent promise like sacrifice is the seed from which the greatest gardens of life bloom. In our lives, sacrifice often feels like a test and sometimes a moment where we're asked to choose between what's easy and what's meaningful. Yet, it's in these choices that we discover who we truly are. It's in letting go of our comfort to support someone we love, setting aside personal desires to fulfill a shared vision, or walking the harder path for a cause that ignites our soul. Sacrifice is where we find not only strength but purpose. The most courageous hearts are the ones that choose to give, even when it's hard. To sacrifice is not to diminish but to transcend, to let go of the small in favor of the infinite.

Let sacrifice be a reminder of the strength we carry within, the ability to face hardship and still choose love. It shows us that even when life asks us to give something away, it often gives us something far greater in return: connection, resilience, and a legacy of kindness that will echo long after we're gone.

Sacrifice doesn't weaken us; it builds us. It transforms ordinary lives into extraordinary stories. It teaches us that while the world may value what we gain, the soul finds peace in what we give. And in the end, it's not the things we hold onto that define us, but the lives we touch through our willingness to give.

Chapter 66: Weight of Expectations

Expectations are invisible yet heavy chains that many of us carry through life. They come from every direction, family, society, friends, and even ourselves. While they can motivate and inspire, they often weigh us down, creating a gap between who we are and who we think we should be.

The weight of expectations often begins in childhood, shaped by cultural norms, parental hopes, and societal ideals. "Be successful. Make us proud. Follow this path." These words, often spoken with love, can feel like anchors that tether us to a life we may not have chosen. Over time, the desire to meet these expectations can overshadow our own dreams, leaving us disconnected from our authentic selves.

The greatest burden we carry is not failure, but the fear of failing others. In adulthood, the expectations multiply. Careers must be impressive, relationships must be perfect, and lives must appear flawless. Social media amplifies this pressure, presenting curated glimpses of success that fuel comparison and self-doubt. The truth, however, is that no one is immune to the struggle of expectation. Beneath the surface, everyone carries their own battles and that's some visible, others hidden.

Expectation is a mirror; it reflects what we aspire to, but also what we fear to lose. The journey to lightening this burden begins with self-awareness. Ask yourself: Whose expectations am I carrying? Are they aligned with my values and aspirations? Letting goes of expectations that no longer serve you is not selfish. Free yourself from the prison of others' expectations, and you'll discover a life that's your own.

Life is too short to be lived for others, and too precious to be defined by external standards. The weight of expectations is real, but so is your power to shed it, redefine it, and rise above it. Let your heart, not the world, dictate your worth.

Chapter 67: When Dreams Diverge

The heart knows no map, only the courage to follow. Dreams are deeply personal; they stem from our passions, experiences, and unique perceptions of the world. When someone's vision of the future doesn't match our own, it's not a betrayal but a reminder of the complexity of being human. Each of us carries a story, and every story seeks its own destination. At first, diverging dreams can create tension and a sense of being misunderstood or a fear of losing connection. But this divergence also holds immense potential for growth.

When faced with diverging dreams, conversations become crucial. Open dialogue allows us to understand not only the dreams but the emotions behind them, the fears, hopes, and longings that drive us. Listening with empathy can transform a moment of separation into an opportunity for deeper connection. In the space between two dreams lies the chance to discover a new horizon together. And when dreams part ways, it doesn't mean the love is lost; it means the heart is learning to expand.

The bravest thing you can do is chase your dream, even if it leads you away from the familiar. Ultimately, diverging dreams remind us of life's constant evolution. Paths may split, but the love, memories, and lessons shared remain etched in our hearts. Each dream, whether shared or separate, contributes to the tapestry of who we are.

Dreams may diverge, but the courage to follow them keeps us united in spirit. Honor your path, and trust that those meant to walk with you will find their way to your side.

Chapter 68: Life After Loss

Loss has a way of leaving us breathless, as if the world has shifted, and we're standing on ground that no longer feels solid. Whether it comes through the passing of a loved one, end of any relation or cherished dream that leaves a mark on the human soul can't be heal. Like all we know, in the immediate aftermath of loss, life can feel as though it's suspended in a fog. The world keeps moving, yet time seems frozen for us.

Some questions arise with almost no answer can relief like why did this happen? What now? The wound is the place where the light enters you and in the garden of memory, in the palace of dreams... that is where you and I shall meet. And while searching the answer we often discover new perspectives on life. Healing doesn't mean the damage never existed. It means the damage no longer controls your life.

Those who hold connection such as friends, family, or even strangers who've walked similar paths can provide support, understanding, and a reminder that we are not alone. When someone you love becomes a memory, the memory becomes a treasure. The reality is that you will grieve forever. You will not 'get over' the loss of a loved one; you will learn to live with it. You will heal and you will rebuild yourself around the loss you have suffered. You will be whole again, but you will never be the same. Nor should you be the same, nor would you want to.

We become not just survivors but storytellers, carrying the legacy of what we've lost and weaving it into the fabric of what we are becoming. This is the essence of resilience, the beauty of the human spirit: to rise again, to love again, to live again.

Chapter 69: The Meaning of Commitment

The unseen force that shapes destinies and strengthens hearts. a daily decision to stand by something or someone with unwavering resolve. Commitment transforms fleeting moments into meaningful stories, and it turns dreams into realities. Commitment is doing what you said you would do, long after the mood in which you said it has left you.

Life often tests the strength of our commitments. There will be days when doubt whispers in our ears, when the path feels steep, and when giving up seems easier. But commitment is what keeps us going. It's the inner voice that says You've come this far, so keep moving." It's not what we do once in a while that shapes our lives. It's what we do consistently.

It's the promise we make, not out of obligation, but out of love and purpose. It binds us to our goals, our values, and to each other. It's the bridge between intentions and actions, ensuring that what we cherish in our hearts is reflected in how we live. In relationships, commitment is the glue that holds us together, even when the world pulls us apart. It's not about perfection; it's about persistence. It's showing up for each other in the messy, imperfect moments and saying, that I choose you, every day.

In personal growth, commitment is what pushes us to keep going when the initial excitement fades. It's the discipline to practice, to show up, and to persevere. It reminds us that every great achievement starts with the decision to try and the determination to keep trying. And in our purpose, commitment is the seed from which greatness grows. It fuels innovation, builds resilience, and creates legacies. Without it, dreams remain dreams. With it, they become milestones in the journey of life.

The only limit to your impact is your commitment to the cause. Commitment is also a lesson in humility and strength. It teaches us to embrace the process, to accept setbacks, and to trust that every step matters. It's not about never falling; it's about always rising. But perhaps the most beautiful aspect of commitment is its simplicity: it's a choice. A choice to care, to show up, and to give our best. It doesn't demand perfection, just effort. It doesn't require grand gestures, just consistency.

Stay committed, even when it's hard. The best things in life are worth it. To commit is to honor the essence of life. It's a declaration that says, I believe in this. I believe in you. I believe in myself. It's a gift we give, one that has power to change not just our own lives but the world around us.

In a fleeting world, commitment is timeless. It reminds us that when we dedicate ourselves fully, we create something enduring, something that speaks of love, courage, and the unshakable strength. Commitment doesn't bind us actually it frees us to become who we were meant to be.

Let commitment be your compass, guiding you through the storms and into the light. It's the heartbeat of purpose, the anchor of love, and the foundation upon which extraordinary lives are built.

Chapter 70: A Mother and A Father

The most powerful relationship, a mother and a father is are not just roles they are architects of love, sacrifice, and guidance. Together, they form the first world for us. They can be storytellers, the protectors, and the silent witnesses to every first step, first word and first dream.

A mother embodies the warmth of unconditional love. She is the gentle embrace that soothes pain, the quiet whisper of encouragement when the world feels overwhelming. She is the one who notices the smallest details and knows everything even if you don't tell. And when come to father, he feels everything but doesn't express much as his love may be quieter, less spoken, but it is felt deeply in his actions. He is the encourager, pushing his child to dream bigger, and to stand taller.

Together, they are cure of anything and care for you. Where one nurtures, the other challenges; where one protects, the other empowers. A mother's love is the fuel that enables a normal human being to do the impossible and A father's love is the compass that points a child to their true north.

Yet, being a mother and father is far from easy. It is a journey of sleepless nights, difficult decisions, and endless sacrifices. It's learning to let go while holding on, to guide without controlling, and to love without condition. It is a balancing act of giving all they have while teaching their children to stand on their own. Their actions, values, and love ripple through generations. A mother and a father show their children what it means to care, to persevere, and to believe in something greater than themselves. They are the ones who ground us in an age of distractions, teaching us the value of connection, presence, and purpose.

To the mothers and fathers, your love shapes the world. To the world, you may be one person, but to your child, you are the world. A mother and a father are not perfect but they are more than humans you need daily. The words are less to truly express who they are and what they mean for us.

Chapter 71: Mirror of Nature

Every sunrise carries the promise of renewal, and every storm teaches us resilience. The gentle ripples of a lake remind us how our smallest actions create waves, affecting lives far beyond our immediate circle. Nature is more than scenery; it is a silent teacher, a patient guide, and an enduring mirror that reflects the essence of human existence. Take the forest, for instance. A single tree is strong, but its true power lies in its connection its roots entangle with others, creating a network that supports the entire ecosystem. This mirrors the relationships we cultivate in life. Just as no tree grows in isolation, no person thrives alone. Our strength lies in the connections we nurture and the communities we build.

Nature also teaches us the art of balance. The sun rises, the moon follows, and seasons transition seamlessly, each playing its role without overshadowing the other. This balance is a reminder to harmonize the many facets of our own lives. We are often caught in a tug-of-war between ambition and rest, between giving and receiving. But nature shows us that harmony is not perfection, it is the ability to flow with life's rhythm, embracing every season with grace. Even in chaos, nature inspires like forest got fire, yet from the ashes new life emerges. Isn't this much like our own challenges? The hardest moments often pave the way for growth we never imagined.

As we walk among nature's wonders, we are reminded of simplicity. In every walk with nature, one receives far more than they seek. At last nature is the mirror of the peace and peace nature bring.

Chapter 72: Humanity as Successors on Earth

When we think about humanity's place on Earth, we are often caught between pride in our achievements and the weight of our responsibilities. What our past teaches us, many great has come and gone but humans are still onto their way of not understanding the rights. Where humanity alive people are not and where people are humanity is far away. What we choose to build, protect, and nurture today is taken away from something, the more we are shaping the world, the more we're disconnecting with reality. Every intention people carry are mix of balancing from which we can't move forward.

To be a successor is not simply to inherit, it's to honor and enhance. But the title of "successor" comes with challenges. Have we learned to coexist with the Earth, or are we only beginning to understand the depth of our role? The seas rise, the forests diminish, and the air carries whispers of warning. This is not just an alarm to notice but the calls to awaken to make this world better. We must ask ourselves not what the planet can do for us, but what we can do to leave it thriving for those who follow.

Humanity's strength is not just in innovation what can be done better but the ability to unite every individual and make part of the same story that gives us the chance to redefine what it means to be servant of this earth.

Success is not in domination, but in balance. Let us be the ancestors our successors will celebrate. Not for the monuments we build, but for the wisdom we manifest Because, in the end, to succeed as humanity is to ensure life on Earth continues to thrive, long after we're gone. We do not inherit the Earth from our ancestors; we borrow it from our children. The true measure of humanity is not in what we take from the Earth, but in what we give back to it.

Chapter 73: Courage to Begin Again

Life is an endless cycle of endings and beginnings, each chapter folding into the next with lessons. The courage to begin again is not just about resilience, it's about embracing the unknown with a heart full of hope and a mind open to possibilities. It's about acknowledging the weight of past failures while refusing to let them define the chapters yet to be written.

Those who feel week to begin again as it not the weakness instead testament of strength as it requires stepping into uncertainty with the understanding that growth often lies in discomfort.

In every factor whether it's a new career, a rekindled relationship, or a shift in perspective, every new beginning carries the seeds of new growth. Imagine a tree shedding its leaves each autumn. It doesn't mourn the loss; instead, it gathers strength from its roots, knowing spring will bring new life. Similarly, in moments of starting over, we reconnect with our core, finding strength in who we are.

Every sunset is proof that endings can be beautiful, and every sunrise is a promise that beginnings hold infinite potential. When we muster the courage to start anew, we rewrite the narrative of our lives. Each attempt, no matter how small, is a victory over fear, an act of defiance against doubt. In starting over, we don't erase the past, we honor it by carrying its forward. In every ending lies the promise of a new beginning. The courage to start again is the quiet power that transforms our struggles into stepping stones, guiding us to a future brighter than we ever imagined.

Chapter 74: The Digital Trap

As this starts, do you know what a digital trap really is? You have to get into it. When you connect with different people from different cultures and countries, you learn many things. You meet good as well as bad people, but that all happens in reality too, so what is the difference? What once promised knowledge and connection has, for many, become a trap, unfortunately, that steals away moments of real life.

The digital trap isn't just about the time we spend staring at screens but the cost it exacts on our mental health, relationships, and even our sense of self. The mind repeats all the things you do and it became loop that never end. People scroll endlessly even sometimes don't what actually we're doing seeking validation from everything are left behind like we're getting enough likes, comments and how others are reacting in digital interactions. The lines between reality and online personas blur, leading us to measure self-worth where we believe more in machine then ourselves. Relationships suffer as screens replace eye contact, and meaningful conversations are lost to the buzz of notifications. This trap is not simply technological, it's deeply human that a reflection of our need to belong and to escape.

What actually people do on their phones nobody knows, creating hate, dividing relation, sharing weird stuff, blackmailing, doing illegal things etc. Addiction never ends it just replace with something else. A reminder that stepping away from our screens can bring us closer to the people and experiences that truly matter. Not everyone can bare mental trauma, your every step impact something you don't know. Step outside the digital cage; the world is far more vivid than pixels can show.

The thing is this trap is the first step toward freedom. It takes courage to reclaim the balance, to remember that technology is just a tool and not our master. When used wisely, it can enrich our lives. When misused, it can deplete the essence of what makes us human.

To break free, we must cultivate mindfulness. Pause before reaching for the phone, ask why we're diving into the digital world, and prioritize the moments that truly matter. Step outside, look at the sky, and connect with the world as it is not through a filtered lens, but in its raw, unpolished beauty. The digital world is a window, not the entire view. Step back, open the door, and experience life without the screen between.

Those who architects digital age, are those who often find themselves trapped in it that they have built. A device in every hand and yet loneliness rises, perhaps because connection through wires can never replace the warmth of a human touch. We were born into a world of wonder, yet we've confined ourselves to screens.

It's a challenge, one that calls us to be conscious and intentional. As we learn to step back, we begin to remember what it means to live fully and authentically, outside the flickering glow of our devices. To protect humanity from digital trap we have to master ourselves that what we made can't control us.

Chapter 75: Prognosticate the Unknown

The future is a blank canvas that still needs to be painted which is both scary as well as exciting. We all know that we can't directly see the future but we can hope for something that could happen. It is about us as human beings that we look into the future and we are not prepared to what is coming in reality.

Expansion of consciousness is one such possibility. Where we're integrating our minds with technology, which would enable us to reach places in our mind that we haven't even thought off, or even better, link minds that have never been linked before! While such a thought might serve of opening new levels of knowledge, it also raises the age-old question of humanity.

The future may include life beyond Earth. Any day you can see shows where humans moving to places like Mars, leaving Earth behind. As technology improves every year, we might live in other galaxies someday, bringing both our strengths and flaws with us. In the next 10–20 years, technology could take us to places we've only imagined.

Changes in the environment can often be seen even close to where we live. Issues like ancient diseases reappearing or the effects of climate change show how powerful nature is. Snow falls in places where we never see it, and it would vanish from places where it currently snows. These challenges remind us of the Earth's strength and may push us to find new ways to live and adapt, all while treating the environment with care and respect.

Many people see time as constant, but I think it doesn't have to be that way. The way we understand time is more complex than science explains. We can be in the future anytime as learning from the past becomes easy, and today, the intellect of humans predicting the future will make this happen soon.

Chapter 76: Symphony of Simplicity

Whenever you think you're not interesting, you risk becoming boring simply by believing it. Simplicity is not boring; it's quality. Only a few people hold what makes you different and unique from everyone. If you not doing what every like to do then you're special. a way of living that invites us to strip away the noise and focus on the essence of life. In the modern world, where distractions are constant and complexity often celebrated, simplicity feels like a lost. Yet, it is in simplicity that we find peace and clarity.

Simplicity isn't about having less; it's about living more. It's the quiet strength of knowing what to hold onto and what to release. It's the freedom of letting go of the unnecessary to make room for the extraordinary. Simplicity magnifies the small things that make life beautiful. A child's laughter, a shared meal, or the sound of leaves rustling in the wind, these are the moments that bring depth and warmth to our days. Simplicity teaches us that fulfillment is not found in more but in enough. It reminds us that happiness isn't something to be chased; it's something to be lived, here and now.

Choosing simplicity in today's world quite difficult, we step away from the noise and into a life filled with clarity and purpose. It's not about denying ourselves but about honoring what truly matters. In the quiet of simplicity, we hear the truth of our souls. A simple life is not devoid of joy but overflowing with meaning.

Let simplicity be a song we carry within us, a reminder that life's most profound gifts often come in the quietest of moments. In this symphony, we find not only peace but a way of being that is deeply, beautifully human.

Chapter 77: Way to the Heaven

We have come so far; the concept of heaven is not as easy as we think. A destination everyone wants to be there, but nobody knows who will be. Our hearts attached to it, which is a realm of peace, joy, and boundless love. It's not just a place but a state of being a reflection of how we treat others. How truly our intentions are towards other.

In our quest for heaven, we often look upward, imagining celestial realms. But what if the way is inward? What if the doors to heaven are unlocked by compassion, humility, and understanding? Every step we take toward healing a broken heart, uplifting a struggling soul, or standing firmly for justice brings heaven closer to earth.

And those who don't believe, where the question arises like how we know about what we have never seen? Why should I do good for others? What will I get by doing that? All come to believe, have you ever seen your heart? No right, still you agree that it's there in your body; likewise, belief works on faith you have in something. Some people think that I got everything in my life because of my good deeds. Actually, you're not as everyone got things by creator to test you on the different basis. The best thing about life is you never lose anything by providing for others.

The mistakes we make, the pain we endure, and the lessons we learn are all part of the sacred journey. The way to heaven begins when we forgive ourselves and others, allowing the scars of the past to become the wisdom of the present. As we look toward the unknown, let us remember that heaven is not simply a destination to be reached; it is a way of life to be lived. The path lies within each of us, ready to light up with every choice that aligns us with goodness, truth, and unity.

Heaven is not above the clouds but within the hearts of those who dare to live with love and purpose.

Chapter 78: Something you Need to Listen

In the world that constantly pushes you to be more and more to be perfect but the reality is you were never meant to be perfect, you were meant to be real. We often live as if tomorrow is guaranteed, putting off the things that truly matter. Nobody knows the tomorrow; things are unexpected and anything can happen just next sec.

Many fears of failing perhaps, failure is the only true teacher life has to offer. Learn to see failures as steps on the ladder to success. Never thought kindness as weakness it's the quiet strength that binds humanity together and Take time to nourish your soul, to sit in silence, and to reconnect with who you are beyond the roles you play.

Try to improve and make changes because when everyone is ill, they find fault in something else, and when just you're ill, they find fault inside you. Adapt yourself to places that make you stronger and think like you want to become because everything starts from your mind. What you think inside your head you become and you're what you think about. And the rest of the thing is left in the hands of your creator because nobody knows you better than your creator.

Life isn't a solo act; one beautiful heart is greater than many beautiful faces. Life is good without more social interactions; learning is a different concept to be yourself, what you observe, and deliver. Sometimes you have to sacrifice something to win the game. What life is, either use that thing wisely, and it will win for you.

Always be humble because I've seen people become what they once laughed at. It's better to be unique than the best, as unique makes you the only, and the best can be many; you just have to be crazy enough to think that's possible. Sometimes opinions hurt people, but they defend them instead of improving. Take it as challenge to prove yourself.

Chapter 79: The End of Beginning

We are almost here to end this journey of chapters about what we're doing on earth, and if you read it all, then congratulations. Every journey has a destination or we say the end, yet the truth of life is that every ending is simply a doorway to something new, a beginning we might not yet fully understand. As this is last chapter of this book let us reflect not just on the words written, but on the stories, we carry within us.

This book has been mirror reflecting of human experience our struggles, triumphs, questions, and hopes. Every chapter was a step deeper into understanding what it means to be alive. But what now? What lies beyond this final page? The answer is you.

The story of life is not confined to the pages of a book. It breathes in your actions, your choices, your dreams, your decisions, your intentions, and mostly your perspective on how you look at yourself and people around you. The end of the book is the beginning of the reader's journey. Life is full of cycles. It is not the chapters we read but the chapters we live that define us.

This book was never about answers but about questions life asks us. Now, the pen is in your hand. Write boldly, live fully, and never stop seeking the extraordinary in the ordinary. Remember, you are not alone in this journey, and together, we are part of countless stories on earth.

As you close this book, take a deep breath and step forward with hope. Nothing ends, as end is the new beginning, like how goodbye is the new hello, and so this is not goodbye, but rather a heartfelt invitation to keep going. What we're doing on the earth to What we're becoming on the Earth.

The journey continues, always.

Acknowledgment

Writing What We're Doing on Earth is started as a little corner of excitement for me as it now has made me come across some of the best moments people lived through and some of the worst. But, most importantly, the potential that we have. The lines that I have written in this book are not only mine, they belong to everybody around the world.

I am extremely thankful to every person who believed in this one and inspired me to complete it. You are the heart of this book.

I would like to thank my audience for being on this ride with me and for their encouragement. Your interest, your thought, and your demand to understand the true purpose of our existence on this earth appreciates every single word written in the pages of the book. I also wish to thank my family, friends and everyone who motivated me to be original and show the world what I can do by my words.

After five months of journey, I've reached here. Now, I'd love to hear from you! Your thoughts, big or small, mean the world to me. If you could take a moment to share a review, feedback, or even just a favorite chapter, it would mean so much. Let me know what *you're* doing on Earth because your story matters too. FYI, 20% of the content is included using AI.

Feel free to drop me a message or share your thoughts on any platform. Together, let's keep the conversation alive. All in all, let us change, let us bond and let us appreciate this earth that we live in. **– Your Radiant**

With gratitude and hope,

Fardeen Khan

Stay connected:

Email – yoursradiant@gmail.com

Insta - https://www.instagram.com/fardeen_k3/

X - https://x.com/Yoursradiant

THE END

Copyright Page

What We're Doing on Earth
Copyright © 2024 by Fardeen Khan

This book is a work of the author's imagination and research. Any resemblance to actual persons, living or dead, events, or locales is purely coincidental unless otherwise noted.

First Edition: 2024

For permissions or inquiries, contact: khanfardeen8828@gmail.com

9 798230 904502